Travers, Mary, 1936-200
Mary Travers : a
woman's words /
2013.
33305230951356
mi   12/30/14

S0-AVR-163

Mary Travers

A Woman's Words

With
MIKE RENSHAW

No part of this book may be used or reproduced in any manner whatsoever without the written permission of Renshaw Associates LLC. Cover photograph by The Associated Press. Back cover photograph by Robert Corwin/robertcorwin.com.

Copyright© 2013 Renshaw Associates LLC
All rights reserved.
ISBN: 149287129X
ISBN 13: 9781492871293

Library of Congress Control Number: 2013919125
CreateSpace Independent Publishing Platform
North Charleston, South Carolina

Mary Trump

Contents

About This Book

Mary Travers (1936-2009) was America's premier female folk voice soon after she began singing professionally in the turbulent 1960s. But her inspiring expression was not limited to a remarkable musical talent; her passion for social justice and equality was also reflected in newspaper columns, unpublished essays, speeches, stage monologues, and poetry.

This work is a collection of her views on her life and political times. This compilation is a joint effort with her long-time friend and editor, Mike Renshaw, a veteran Pennsylvania journalist and Emmy-winning television producer and a former president of the Philadelphia chapter of the Society of Professional Journalists. His work has appeared in various publications including The Philadelphia Inquirer and The New York Times.

■

You'll see many references in these pages to "Noel." Noel "Paul" Stookey is the Paul of Peter, Paul and Mary.

Dedication

For Virginia and Lila

Foreword

BY PETER YARROW

Mary was always reading.

At rehearsals, snatching moments between her turn at making up a vocal part for a song, reading as we piled into a limo to take us to a concert hall, reading backstage when she was called to warm up, and even reading when we were discussing whether to perform for some march or demonstration – lifting up her head only to venture an opinion, say "great," or offering a pithy and direct analysis to let us know why, or why not, she felt we should participate.

Today, we call this multitasking, but then it was simply part of Mary being Mary – ever more informed than either Noel or me on a huge panoply of issues and areas of history, literature, philosophy, science, and more science. Mary was always fascinated with the how and the why of life. She loved the science section of *The New York Times* and each week waited for it with great anticipation.

Mary was in love with the printed page and more than anyone I ever knew seemed to be able to literally go to another place, in heart and mind, when she read. Frequently on the road, she would turn to Noel and me when we were in a car or backstage in rehearsal before a show and read a sentence or a turn of a phrase that struck her as beautifully crafted or powerfully stated.

She honored and fairly worshiped the carefully chosen words that Sister Mary Corita wrote or quoted on her silk-screen prints, some of which Mary collected and hung in her home, such as the iconic print, "I should like to be able to love my country and still love justice – Camus"

In Noel's and my opinion, Mary was always right on target in these moments when she shared a line, passage, or phrase from what she was reading. Much as she had an unerring ear for a song that would suit us because it told a story that was in our hearts to tell, she never failed to pick out the gems of literature created by a writer that had, at least for the moment, stolen her heart.

Mary loved to write.

Sometimes, when we would ask her to do so, she wrote poems that told the story of Peter, Paul and Mary's most recent chapter of our life together – encapsulating it in a few lines that were both graceful and powerful, as memorable as they were elective, words carefully chosen that always seemed to flow from her pen with unstudied ease.

It was Mary who, in such writings, gave our audiences a glimpse of the personal as well as musical road we had traveled and a feeling for what had energized our journey.

Mary captured the essence of what we were trying to communicate as people, in our music and in our activism, sometimes in the dedication of an album, or later a CD, a note of sympathy for a friend who had endured a loss, or a note to someone we wanted to thank for the gift of assistance or insight that had helped us be better advocates for our mutually held passions: justice, fairness, equity, and peace.

Her words were always surprising and highly individual and, unlike the songs whose lyrics we dissected and tweaked before singing them, we never changed a single word, comma, or title of any of Mary's poems.

We didn't need to. They were always perfect.

Mary also wrote about the world at large: its struggles, its problems, its injustices, its triumphs, and sometimes its lyrical beauty, which, though we shared remarkable experiences together, she also acquired and wrote about her own special vision and passions, apart from those of the group.

Many of these works were shared with Mike Renshaw, a great friend of Mary's and of the trio who, knowing that although Mary was an extremely gifted writer, also knew that, as a high school dropout (though in her life experience had earned at least the equivalent two Ph.D.s in literature), she was missing the multiplication tables of some of the skills that could transform her writings into superbly crafted op-ed pieces, narrative pieces, or reflections on her own life. Many of the writings that became op-ed submissions were published in several newspapers, including *The New York Times.* Many of the narrative pieces that she wrote were not published, but now, they are.

Mike loved and respected Mary as a gifted artist and a dear friend, and he admired her knowledge, wit, keen sense of literature, and her most personal and creative use of the English language. She loved learning from him and delighted in the literary tug-of-war that is a big part of the writer-editor relationship.

For more than 25 years, Renshaw was her trusted editor and confidant. They began working together when he was editor of the *Bucks County Courier Times*, a daily newspaper in suburban Philadelphia.

Mike is an accomplished writer himself, and we collaborated on the song, *Fair Ireland*, recorded on the CD *Flowers and Stones.* He wrote the lyrics and I, the music. He was also my editor on articles I published in *The Wall Street Journal* and *The New York Times.*

With Mike, Mary realized one of her greatest dreams: to become, in her off-stage life, one who emulated and embraced the legacy of her parents' gifts. Virginia and Robert Travers were both distinguished writers and journalists in their time.

Mary's published op-ed pieces were much talked about, highly respected, and in terms of their effect, took their place in the cosmos of the sometimes small, individual acts that one puts forth to try to make the world a better place. Other unpublished pieces that appear in this volume of Mary's writings are arguably equally powerful, insightful, and poetic.

With Mike Renshaw's skillful and respectful hand, Mary's writings acquired greater impact and a more focused edge.

They were quite the team.

This volume of Mary's words, from newspaper columns to speeches, to poetry, to radio commentary, to her delightful on-stage monologues, will bring you closer to the kind of awareness that Noel Paul, I, and some of Mary's closest friends were fortunate enough to acquire.

Through Mary's words, you will get to know some of the many facets of her prodigious talents that you may have suspected truly existed but could not have known until now were part of her gift to those she loved and, now through this book, to the world.

Finally, Mary wrote prose and stories, and, at one point, she also began to write chapters about her life that told of the experiences that shaped her personality and fostered the growth of her ethical perspective, empathy, and compassion – traits for which she was widely acknowledged. In particular, her writings about her family's African-American maid, Lila, a wise, no-nonsense, yet gentle and loving woman who inspired Mary and helped to bring her up, reveal Mary's earliest discoveries about the nature and existence of justice and injustice.

Lila's chapter is a micro-tale that complements Mary's very famous and resolute dedication and contributions to the civil-rights movement. Later, the women's movement and other grass-roots advocacies became the focus of her personal commitment and direct participation. Over time, as the Peter, Paul and Mary years passed, such efforts became more a way of life than a short-lived perspective for all three of us.

For those of you who have heard Mary, the singer, the powerful and charismatic force on stage, and the articulate spokesperson for public issues, this book will let you see, feel, and hear the complex and questioning nature of the inner workings of Mary's intellect and soul.

There was much more to Mary than the public ever knew, particularly the wit and humor with which she expressed herself, not only in her solos on stage, but in everyday life.

Mary's word magic sparkled in the solo performances of our concerts. She would poke fun at herself, at the craziness of the world, and at the notions of modernity that continued to baffle her.

Enjoy her words in all their forms.

Let her inspire you as she has Noel Paul and me, and may this book become one of your favorite places to go when you need a dose of down-home clarity and a humane, unromanticized balance in your life

CHAPTER 1

Lila and the Mink Coat

I've always wanted to write about Leila Turner, or as I called her, Lila.

She was the black woman who raised me and who had a profound effect on my life. Times change, as do perceptions and interpretations of a moment in time, but our memories of childhood resist contemporary interpretations.

I grew up in a racist society among people who did their best to overcome racism. While I've always wanted to write about Lila, I put off doing it, fearing I would be accused of being too sentimental, old-fashioned, and even racist. I am very probably all those things, no matter how I try not to be.

But I loved Lila, and she loved me. My gratitude has outgrown my timidity.

She saved me. She rescued me from what would have been a hurtful and damaging inheritance.

We had come to Greenwich Village from Schenectady, New York, in 1939. My mother was all of 22 and I, a tow-headed three-year-old. My parents had just separated, and my mother, a journalist, had just found a job at a newspaper. Someone would have to take care of me, and so Lila came into my life. She was our grown-up.

1

Lila was already 40 and had three children and two grandchildren. She was born in Virginia, married there, and moved to New York with her husband, Willie. They lived on "The Hill," Sugar Hill in Harlem.

The Hill was where the middle class and wealthy blacks lived in New York. It was a real neighborhood then, easy and proud of its quiet, clean streets and unlocked doors. Edgecomb Avenue overlooked the park with its two swimming pools and playground.

Its residents thought themselves set apart from the poorer parts of Harlem, but not immune to the poverty. They were, most of them, the first generation of their families to penetrate the edges of the American dream in relative safety. I remember Harlem as a lovely sunny neighborhood full of warm, dark adults.

And Lila made it home.

Hers was a large apartment – three bedrooms, a dining room, and an eat-in kitchen. The dining room served as the master bedroom for Lila and Willie. Its walls were covered with framed pictures of black men and women who had made it in sports and the arts. Pictures not of people Lila and Willie knew, but of people who made Lila and Willie proud.

Lila Turner and husband Willie. (Travers Estate Photo)

Their home was an old apartment building, with graying, worn marble stairs and the mixed scents from countless meals that permeated the halls. They were always cool and dim. I suspect that the landlord didn't use anything above 40 watts.

When I remember my childhood, it is always: 148th Street and Edgecomb Avenue. So much happy family time for a child with so little of her own ... how I miss the conductor of my escape from my mother's despair, Lila.

My mother, so young then, younger in some ways than anyone can survive being. She had been raised in the South, by her grandmother, after her mother had committed suicide when she was six. Her father was unknown and never mentioned. Great Uncle Clyde supported his mother and his niece, as a traveling salesman. There was never enough of anything, but in especially short supply was simple physical warmth. When Clyde could no longer support two houses, one in the South and one in the North, my mother, then 12, and her grandmother moved to Albany, New York, to stay with Clyde.

My mother speaks of a lonely and displaced childhood, but junior high school presented her with an English teacher who would inspire and encourage her. Praise was finally possible, although a bit late. At 15, she became a newspaper reporter, at 18 a bride, and at 19, a mother. By 22, she was separated.

She had married a man not unlike herself.

Robert Travers was a young reporter she'd met at the newspaper. He had been an orphan too, dependent on the charity of relatives. A good man who was too hard on himself and others. Intimacy for the two of them was difficult, trust perhaps years away. They parted, knowing that they had failed each other and me. They gave only what their circumstances had taught them to give. I was of different, more selfish, stuff, and I had Lila.

She was little, small-boned, light-skinned with freckles and green eyes. A face with the nose and cheekbones of America's first settlers, the Indians. Her forebears were African, Cherokee, and Irish. The conquered and the conqueror, each in their own time, gave her face and her character a sense of genetic survival.

She was a true matriarch.

The beginning

When Lila first came to work for my mother, we were living on MacDougal Street in Greenwich Village. The Village was fundamentally an Italian neighborhood, set amidst the architecture of old, sturdy stone and brick houses and working-class apartment buildings. We had rented one of two twin Early American brownstones. Their fronts were graced by attractive, black, wrought-iron-filigreed frames.

Next door was probably New York's last open-forge blacksmith. He made decorative fireplace accessories. I remember, I must have been four or five, going into his dark workshop and standing small and quiet, staring at him pumping his bellows, blowing sparks that danced into the chimney hood. It was a place of mystery and excitement. When I was grown, I visited the steel mills in Pennsylvania and felt the same sense of awe, to watch man mold the earth's rawest of elements.

Across the street was a newspaper stand run by a neighborhood Italian fellow; it's still there. Once, my mother had occasion to use its neighborhood telegraph. Some boys had shot out one of our front windows with a BB gun.

She knew who fired the gun, and she notified the man at the newspaper stand that she was going to swear out a warrant for the kid's arrest. By that evening, there was a knock at our door, and the young man and his elder brother stood there. They had come to apologize. The elder of the two boys assured my mother that his brother would never do such a thing again if my mother could see her way not to press charges. For months after, when my mother came down the street with her groceries, boys sprang out of doorways and down from street corners to carry her packages. From then on, our house was protected by an unseen but very real neighborhood presence, decidedly Sicilian.

Lila loved the Village, whose culture and she had one thing in common, the belief that little girls should appear in public in heavily starched dresses and pinafores. I changed clothes two or three times a day, much to the neighborhood ladies' approval. Lila loved shopping in the Village. The fresh vegetable stands on Bleecker Street were reasonably priced, and the variety and quality were the best in the city. Often she would do her food shopping downtown and ride home with it all the way to Harlem on the subway. The difference in prices and quality between A&P in the Village and the one in Harlem were shocking.

When my great-grandmother came for a long visit, a quiet battle began. Great-grandma was a frail, white-haired lady with lace collars and cameos and a temperament that was as unbending as it was bigoted. She was a great believer in "people knowing their place."

Every night when Lila served dinner, just before going home to her own family, Mrs. Copeland would comment on the evening meal. "Oh, Lila, you make such good chicken" or whatever was being served, "You must have a little white in you."

My great-grandmother knew Lila's grandfather was white and with a deadly Southern code, used her seemingly innocuous comment to illustrate what she believed to be Lila's mongrel parentage.

Lila was not thrilled with Mrs. Copeland's evening attacks and asked my mother to tell her off. My mother, who would have dearly loved to herself, said, "Be my guest."

The battle, unbeknownst to great-grandma, was about to be waged.

Dinnertime came, and we sat down. Lila had made, and I dream of them still, Parker House rolls. Great-grandma looked up and delivered the by-now-expected line: "Oh Lila, you make such good bread, you must have a little white in you."

Lila smiled sweetly. "Why Mrs. Copeland, it's funny you should say that. I do. My grandmother was white."

There was a stunned and tight-lipped silence for the rest of the meal. Lila had lied. It was a small lie, but for a Southerner, it was a devastating anathema.

Lila had said it was her grandmother, not her grandfather, who was white, implying that a white woman had slept with a black man. Great-grandma saw nothing disturbing in the product of the slaveholders' privilege, assuming that a black woman had been taken by a white man. For her, that was a fact of life. But the other was a mortal sin.

She informed my mother at the end of the meal that either Lila went or she did. My mother finally had her moment when she informed her grandmother that one of them was dispensable – and it wasn't Lila.

For a while, it was a stalemate.

Stalemate and peace

The two women carefully avoided each other, but eventually great-grandma went back to live with her son, and peace reigned again.

It was a hard time economically, with about a third of my mother's salary going to Lila. There wasn't much loose change about. But Lila found what there was.

There was an old, rather shabby overstuffed chair in the living room. My mother began to notice that whenever there were male visitors, Lila would insist that they sit in that chair. After a while, she learned that the angle of the seat was such that any loose change in a gentleman's pocket would fall out between the cushions.

My mother, the innocent, would ask Lila to seat them in the better chair. But there was method to Lila's stubbornness about that chair. Between the bottle deposit money and the generosity of what was uncovered when the seat cushion was lifted, Lila and I would go to the Laff Movie.

The Laff Movie was on 14th Street, just off Broadway. It showed 32 color cartoons and two or three shorts – the Three Stooges, Buck

Mom: Virginia with Clyde, her Cavalier King Charles Spaniel. (Travers Estate Photo)

Rogers, or sometimes a western. Sometimes we would spend the whole day there, seeing the entire bill two or three times. Sometimes, when the chair failed to come up with movie money, we would spend our lunch money.

On those days, we would lunch for free, dining on the edible samples in the food department stores on 14th Street – Herns, Klines, and Ohrbachs. Hors d'oeuvre-size bites of cheese and salami and ham slices, then some cookies, seemed a perfectly good lunch to me.

Sometimes we'd "go to Europe."

Lila, who couldn't write very well, was a voracious reader of whatever she found in our house. Faulkner, F. Scott Fitzgerald, Hemingway. She called them her "dirty" books. Her imagination was highly developed

7

and literate. Those books colored our play. Once a week we "went to Europe" on the Staten Island Ferry. There and back on the same nickel.

While we sailed the ferry, it became a sleek and opulent ocean liner, we its passengers. She would spin out a dream story of what I would wear, who was at the ball, and what everyone else was wearing. I visited a Europe of a century past with Lila as my guide. I laugh to think that my socially conscious mother was being slightly undermined by a definitely bourgeois, upwardly mobile black woman.

For Lila, window-shopping was a serious business.

Wedding cakes were compared and judged. Only the best for Mary. Fur coats dismissed as not good enough. Once in a childish, and I see now, condescending tone, while standing in front of a fur store window, I told Lila that when I was older I would give her all of my old mink coats. She teased me about that for years, long past the time that I understood how a white child patronizing her must have made her feel. But she forgave me.

The war years had their own flavor to a child.

My father was away most of the time at sea. He had joined the Merchant Marine in '39 and now sailed as a first mate. All I can remember of him then was how handsome and tall he was in his dark blue uniform with its gold braid and that he'd bring me violets set within a white paper doily, no matter what the season. He was a mystery then and one I spent most of my adult life trying to understand.

The weekends for my single mother were solved when Lila began taking me to her house. I loved it there. There were lots of children, friends of Lola and Bobby, Lila's grandchildren who lived with her. It was a busy apartment with friends and relatives in and out.

There was Pal, a large and very unfriendly police dog. I soon discovered the price of his friendship. Late at night, I'd get up and feed him, piece by piece, a whole loaf of bread. When the air raid sirens would go off, Pal would leap to the window. Standing on the hassock, he'd put his large wolf-like head out the window, and his primitive beginnings would echo as his chilling howl would rise and fall with the siren.

I'd drive Bobby crazy; I loved his toys. He was several years older than I, and in love with metal model airplanes. He had quite a collection and was very protective of them. Everyday he'd hide them from me, and I would spend the day looking for them. Sometimes they would be under the bed, other times I'd have to get on a chair to find them, on top of the built-in armoire. But inevitably, he'd come home from playing ball or hanging out with his friends to find me on the floor with his treasures.

Fortunately for me, Bobby was fundamentally good-natured and of short memory. He certainly was long-suffering. I had found an old piece of curtain lace, and armed with a broom stick as the minister, I'd beg Bobby to marry me, sometimes four or five times a day. Complaining bitterly, he'd oblige.

Lola, Lila's granddaughter, and I were not too close. Not only was she older than I was, but she had discovered boys. Lila would insist that Lola and Elwood, her boyfriend, take me to the movies with them. Lila may have thought that making a 14-year-old take a 6-year-old on her dates was some sort of prevention, but it also may account for the fact that Lola married Elwood at 16.

I know that Lola was a bit jealous of me, by the way she brushed and braided my hair; she always managed to pull it. It must have been hard to have to share Lila with another child, a white one at that.

Butter, my drug of choice

One of the things that I loved to do with Lila was sit with her while she cooked. During the war, butter was rationed. Most people ate margarine. It came in a pouch, with a little yellow dye button in the center of its unappetizing whiteness. You squished the button and mixed the color around in the bag. It was fun to knead the bag, watching the color go from streaky to uniform. But although I loved to mix it, I would never eat it. Then, as now, my drug of my choice was butter.

Lila would take my mother's precious coupons and buy me butter. All my life there was always a stick of butter in the freezer for me at her house. I can still smell her fresh bread. She used to put it in a bowl, covered with a clean, damp dishtowel, on top of the stove. While it

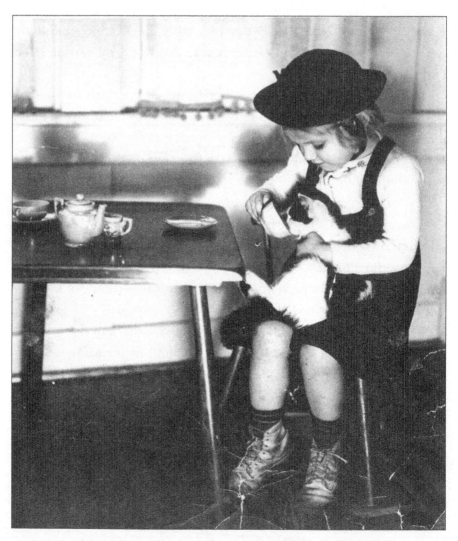

Four-year-old Mary has a tea party with her kitty. (Travers Estate Photo)

rose and was punched down to rise again, she would make the most wonderful codfish cakes. The dried codfish came in a little wooden box. She'd mix the codfish with an egg and mashed potatoes, make the patties, and put them to cool in the refrigerator. When she fried them, they were golden brown and delicious, and they stayed intact. I've tried many times, but mine always fall apart.

Once many years later, when I had my own two children and two stepchildren, Lila came with her great grandson Elwood to my country house in Connecticut. I begged her to make codfish cakes. My stepson Scott's idea of food was hamburgers and hot dogs.

I set the table while Lila cooked. She served everyone but Scott. When he asked her what "that" was, she replied with a disinterested air, "It's not for you, you won't like it."

"But what is it?" his tone peevish.

"I told you it doesn't matter. I am making something else for you."

Lila knew a lot about little boys. Scott ate 10 of Lila's codfish cakes.

Although in the early years, I would go uptown only on weekends, when I was five I got to stay at Lila's for a week when I broke my foot at nursery school. Well, I didn't break it. Some little boy broke it for me. He was trying to move a plank from a sawhorse seesaw when it became too heavy and he dropped it on my foot. There was some argument between Lila and my mother as to whether my foot was really broken. Lila said yes, my mother said I was being dramatic.

I must confess that I always did have a flair for theatrical exaggeration. The doctor settled the dispute with a cast up to my knee. At five, I was long past the stroller stage, but too young to be left alone while Lila shopped. And I was certainly too heavy to carry. So it was no school and uptown for me. Hooray!

Living on the third floor, as they did, proved to be a problem in the fresh-air department. Willie, who had up to then been a bit removed, carried me downstairs and sat with me on the bench across the street. All of his cronies would spend the afternoons standing by the candy store or sitting on the park benches, shooting the breeze. Willie, or Poppa as all his children and grandchildren called him, would sit on the bench each afternoon, and that's where we became friends.

Poppa and his buddies were all baseball fans.

Willie had played in the Negro leagues when he was younger. One afternoon, he took me past the Polo Grounds. Animal lover that I was, I asked where they kept the horses. He gave up on educating me on baseball with that one remark. Later, I did discover the game, but I proved a greater disappointment to him by becoming a Brooklyn Dodgers fan. I was always one for the underdog.

My World War II began with a fight with Lila the Monday after Pearl Harbor. Lila and I were walking to school. For some reason, I was feeling frisky, sometimes another word for rude. I called her a dirty Jap and she chased me all the way to school. And although she had never laid a hand on me, I think she might have that day. I am sure that Lila had been called some racial epithets in her day, but I am equally sure that she never expected that one.

The war years

Harlem during the war was more like the rest of America than midtown New York. But that was true of any ethnic neighborhood. The windows of Harlem displayed flags denoting a son in the armed forces. Although at the beginning of the war, the army was still segregated, the inhabitants of Harlem were as proud of their sons as any Midwesterner.

My mother and I moved from the Village to 64th Street, between Park Avenue and Lexington, when I was seven. She had married a lawyer and had my sister Ann. The apartment house was a large pre-war building with a doorman. Coming from ethnic neighborhoods, black and Italian, Park Avenue was a major culture shock for me.

The children on the block were too well dressed and snooty. I drifted to Third Avenue, which was solid Irish working class. There I met Helen Hunter, who was to be my best friend through high school.

12

Her mother worked as a packer at Bloomingdales and her father drove a beer truck. She had two older sisters and they lived in an apartment next to the El — the elevated subway line that ran up Third Avenue. I used to sleep overnight at Helen's, and at night we'd take a bath in the big tub in the kitchen and would towel-dry next to the large, coal-burning, cast-iron stove.

The icebox was an icebox, and the man brought the ice up the stairs, dripping and slippery clear. The house rumbled every time the train went by, but you got used to it. I used to go to Mass with them every Sunday. My mother was a lapsed Southern Baptist; father had been a lapsed Irish Catholic, so religion was not stressed at home. But at Helen's, sin and redemption were things to be taken seriously.

One Saturday, the Hunters took me to an old-fashioned Irish wake. There was singing and dancing till the wee hours of the morning, with a good deal of booze consumed by the adults. The next morning, despite the late hour that we had gone to bed, we were off, without breakfast, to Sunday Mass. For them, it was communion. For me, it was kneel in the pew and watch the Roman ceremony. The musty, airless smell of the candles and the combination of no sleep and no breakfast overcame me, and while Helen was receiving Jesus, I fainted.

A man vaulted the pew behind me and carried me out to the hall. I woke up in the nun's lap. She had ordered some boy to bring me some water. I drank it and made a face; he had brought Holy Water. So although my mother had been against baptism, I guess the Catholics in the family won out.

Helen and her friends were fun. Her neighborhood, unlike mine, had lots of kids and they were accessible. You knew where they'd be after school. On the street. The walk from my house to Helen's was typical of New York then. You could go from one ethnic group or economic class to another in the space of a few blocks.

Jackie Howard, a friend of Helen's, was my first boyfriend. I invited him to my eighth birthday party. Lila took him aside and asked him

13

to wear a suit. It's true that Jackie was pure boy, dirty face and hands, always tearing his pants climbing on something, but I suspect that Lila was also a bit of a snob.

Jackie to her was a ragamuffin, and as always, Lila wanted better, or at least the illusion of better. Jackie came to my party wearing the only suit he had. A baseball suit. I thought he looked smashing. I did see him once as a grown-up, and his good suit was still a uniform. But this time it was the United States Navy's.

After the birth of my sister, my mother had a nervous breakdown and tried to commit suicide. After having her stomach pumped, she checked herself into a psychiatric hospital in White Plains. My father, who was then a first mate in the Merchant Marine, came home from a run across the wartime Atlantic to discover, to his dismay, that his ex-wife was in the loony bin and his daughter was living with the housekeeper in Harlem.

Lila had taken me home with her and although she wasn't being paid and had no idea when my mother would be well enough to go back to work, she had made the correct assumption that it would all work out.

Dad: Journalist Robert Travers. (Travers Estate Photo)

14

There wasn't a lot of leave time between ships and there was a war going on, so my father was determined to do whatever was the right thing before he had to go back to sea. The thought that he might be torpedoed and leave me uncared for led him to a child psychologist who recommended what was at the time the psychiatric fashion, foster care. He went to lawyers to get the papers drawn up, then went up to the institution where my mother was and explained why she should sign them.

Mental pain is different on different days. The problems that had driven my mother crazy the day she tried to kill herself hadn't gone away, but in the hospital she began to feel better. But when my father said that I should be put in a foster home and thrust the papers in her face, she decided to get well instead. While the storm of her personal pain raged, I was insulated from it all by Lila. I sought love and stability, as all children do, and found it in abundance in a woman who had suffered and survived her own tragedies.

Lila's youngest had been killed accidentally in a street fight. He'd been mistaken for another boy and been stabbed to death. It was a wound that never healed. Sometimes at night, I'd hear her soft sobs, and once when I was very small I climbed into bed with her to comfort her. She held me and patted my small back as I patted hers, and I slept awhile with her that night.

I never recognized my own mother's pain as easily, and when I did, was unable to simply comfort her. I wonder now, was my mother so adept at hiding her pain or was it just too frightening and unsettling for either of us to acknowledge? I suspect that it was both.

The last memory I have of living on 64th Street was a sunny day in 1945. I was in the drugstore on Lexington Avenue, around the corner from my house. It was a wonderful place that had a smell that is now long gone from New York, maybe America. The drugstores then often had food counters, and the combination of the smells from the preparation of prescriptions and the aroma from hot buttered toast was exquisite.

A profound loss

I overheard the druggist talking to the man behind the soda counter: the president, Franklin Delano Roosevelt, was dead. I burst into tears. I was nine years old and he had been president all my life. At nine, I knew that something had changed forever. I left the drugstore and went home and told Lila. For Lila, Roosevelt's death was a profound loss, as if she'd lost a member of her family, and most of America felt that way. Only the grief at John F. Kennedy's death, years later, would be felt so nationally and personally.

At 10, I was back in the Village. I loved it. Greenwich Village was sunny with its low skyline and was perfect for strolling. An important part of any child's development is the need for autonomy. In a walkable village, there is opportunity for unstructured visual stimulation, and a child's imagination has lots to feed on. Greenwich Village was certainly that. There was the park with its chess players and strolling Italian musicians. Or the three blocks of outdoor vegetable stands on Bleecker Street, Italian coffee bars, Catholic churches, street festivals. I walked my dog through the Village and I knew I belonged. I was a respected citizen, certainly not a tourist.

I had always gone to small progressive schools, grown up with the voices of Paul Robeson and Lila's family. My mother and her friends were well aware of the evils produced by prejudice against Jews and blacks. But it was in Harlem that my first lesson in racial animosity was learned.

I was staying at Lila's for the weekend and had gone down to the corner on an errand. Coming back up the hill from 145th Street, I saw a man leaning against a wall with a cute dog. I knew that one should always ask if you can pet someone's dog, so I did. He told me I didn't belong there and I should go home. I hardly heard what he said, for his tone of voice was so angry and threatening, that it produced instant tears.

No one had ever spoken to me with such hostility. I ran up the block, up the stairs to Lila. When I had calmed down enough to repeat

Her first professional photo studio appearance when she was seven. (Travers Estate Photo)

what it was that he'd said, Lila sat me down and explained. "Honey, that man was just hurt. Some white person hurt his feelings and he was just taking it out on you. Don't pay it no mind. It's not you he's angry at." I wonder how many black children have heard the same explanation given to them about a bitter white adult. Had Lila been offered that same consolation when she'd been a child?

As I became a teenager, the trips uptown to Lila's became fewer. I had friends to play with on the weekends, but I continued to go up from time to time. And Lila continued to come downtown, mostly to clean and do the wash and iron. Of all the household jobs, the two she rather liked were ironing and polishing what little silver we had.

She always sang when she ironed – *The Old Rugged Cross*, *What A Friend We Have In Jesus*, and other traditional Baptist hymns. She was the only person in my family who sang. Although my Great Uncle

Clyde said that his mother had led a church choir back in Pigget, Arkansas, when he'd been a boy, I never heard songs at home except from Lila and on the Victrola. Yes, that's what it was called back then.

When I was 14, Lila took a temporary part-time job up the street, for a couple who had just had a baby. She was nearing retirement and wasn't working full-time at our house. One day she came to work saying that she wasn't going to work for those people anymore. "I can't believe some people's ignorance. The husband started to show me how to do the wash ... show *me*. Why, I've been doing the wash for longer than he's been here." She paused and said laughing, "Then he tells me to separate the colors. The whites from the colored." "I told him I've been doing that all my life. But he didn't get it." Mother and I laughed with her, and the story folded itself into Lila lore.

School was always an alienating experience for me. I was always trying to fit in, but I felt odd to myself and I suppose that came across to the other kids. It really didn't get bad until high school, when the combination of my inability to compete scholastically and being the tallest in the class made me a social outcast. If I had been a daydreamer before, I had always believed that it was my choice. Now the high school cliques made it quite clear that it was not my choice but my necessity.

I felt driven inside myself. I read all the time, escaping into other people's worlds, when my own reality became too thin for survival.

High school had become a torture. It was a good school, small with good teachers, but high school was where all my educational failures came home to roost. I didn't even know my multiplication tables. I still don't. To do math problems I'd multiply by the five times table and add the extra numbers. I knew the fives because you needed them to play hide and seek. I froze on tests to the point where I wouldn't try. All I could and would do was read.

I read history books cover to cover, but couldn't see it or remember it broken into chapters. I was an educational disaster waiting for the ax to fall. And, of course, it eventually did. Private schools were loath to fail you, and they didn't believe in leaving you back. So from year to year, I kept going forward while falling further and further behind. Finally, in my junior year, the school heads decided that there was no way they could graduate me. No one knew about learning disabilities then, but I suspect that that was my problem. But the school tried to get to the bottom of the problem using the tools of the time. They insisted I see a therapist, but that didn't help so they gave up. Giving up meant expelling me.

Me and music

Bob DeCormier, my chorus teacher, fought for me. But to no avail. I was out. He came to me and told me he didn't want to lose touch and would I join his outside chorus, "The Young Jewish Folksingers." I did. Music was beginning to look like a lifeline. Bob had been one of those teachers that every student should have in every subject but is lucky to have in one. He was a man who truly had an obvious and palpable passion for music, and his students responded to it. He played us, taking us deep into the music, wrenching out for us far more than could be expected, because he made us feel his sense of awe.

I had my first professional singing experience through him. In the 10th grade, he put together a small group of singers to do a record for Folkways Records with Pete Seeger. One record turned into three — the flip sides to "Talking Union," "Folksongs of Four Continents," and "Bantu Choral Folksongs." We often rehearsed in my house. I lived right across the street from the school, and, of course, because I was so close and thought I had time, I was always late.

When I left, I was crushed. Torture though school was, I had adapted to its pain, so the raw sense that whatever kind of net it had been was gone, and it terrified me. I went to public school for six months. It was a huge school. I had been used to small schools with small classes. Washington Irving was a very large school.

19

A teenager living in the Village. (Travers Estate Photo)

In some classes, I was, for the first time in my life, at the head of the class, merely because I was a ravenous consumer of books. The English teacher didn't care that I couldn't spell. I was reading and liking *Moby-Dick*. I could sing and talk about Elizabethan ballads ... but math was math, public or private. It remained incomprehensible. And so after six months of the eleventh grade, my formal education was over.

For years, not having graduated or gone to college made me feel stupid and inferior. It wasn't till I was 30 that I began to realize that by continuous reading I had gone beyond most of my classmates. They had stopped reading when school ended. I had kept going.

Young people distance themselves from their parents, and I was no different. At 17, I had my first apartment, and for several years I began the real road to growing up. Independence and irresponsibility were easier to survive when an apartment could be found for $42.50 a month.

I always seemed able to find work. I was a dental assistant, a waitress, and a switchboard operator for a small business. I didn't have any really marketable skills, but I wasn't too perturbed about it. Somehow I thought it would all work out, a feeling Lila encouraged.

It was a time of absolute anxiety for my mother. She had despaired of having any affect on the direction that my life was taking. It was not a close time for us. I felt that I had stepped away from the circle of family, and, as in a school vacation, I lived in a state of suspended reality.

When I was 22, I met a young writer, John Filler, who had recently come to New York from California. He was, I thought, exotic. He had been born in Hawaii, came from a military family, and had been a pilot in the Air Force. His roots were totally alien. He was sullen and distant. In my immaturity, I confused these qualities with strength.

We took an apartment on the lower East Side, five flights up. I became pregnant and I didn't want an abortion. He said he wasn't ready for marriage and a baby. He wasn't. But he did the honorable thing, after lots of lobbying from his family and me. At six months, I made an interesting-looking bride.

There is no state of being to match the self-absorption of a young woman pregnant for the first time. John was drifting out as I was zeroing in.

We moved into a three-flight walk-up on MacDougal Street in Greenwich Village. Walking three flights was easier than five, but what was happening inside the apartment was harder. John clearly felt trapped and began to act violently. One night, when the baby was a month old, he came home, lost his temper and hit me so hard that he knocked me clear across the kitchen.

Lila knew that there wasn't much money, since John had lost his job. She had taken to coming downtown and stopping at 14th Street, buying a few things for the baby before coming to visit. She would sometimes bring or make lunch and, looking around the tiny cramped apartment, muse aloud. "Well, you might as well let me do some of the baby's ironing, I never taught you how, and we can't have her looking like an orphan." So while she pressed little dresses, I washed floors – that was my specialty and I confessed my unhappiness. When I told her that John had hit me, she got angrier than I'd ever seen her. She told me that if he did it again, I should lock him out. "When men begin to hit women, they don't stop," she advised me.

She waited that day till John came home and she sent me down to the store for milk. I don't know what she said to him, but he was sullen and quiet that night. She started coming more often. He started staying out nights. The marriage was deteriorating fast. Everyone knew it wouldn't last. My mother wondered how I was going to manage. She hoped for a miracle. Lila was confident that I would be one.

Their hopes came close enough in Peter, Paul and Mary.

Folk music, which had always been for me an esoteric hobby, was beginning to be heard in coffee houses across the country. It had even reached into the pop music world of radio. But no one thought that it would be mainstream. In the midst of my marital disaster came

Riding on Shelter Island, Long Island circa 1955. (Photo by Dan Weiner/Copyright John Broderick)

an opportunity totally misread by me. I had met Noel Paul Stookey when he had first come to New York from Birmingham, Michigan. He was working as a stand-up comedian right across the street from my apartment on MacDougal. He played guitar, and after I told him that I sang a little, he offered to accompany me whenever I wanted to do a guest set at the Gaslight Café, where he worked. I had no desire to sing professionally, but I had some need to say I existed. Music had always served that need.

I met Peter Yarrow through friends; he wanted to put a group together. I introduced him to Noel Paul, and we began to rehearse. For me, it was a project. Everyone in the Village had one, it was their identity. The waitress was an actress, the espresso operator was a writer, the busboy a painter. So Peter, Paul and Mary became my project. I did not believe that a project had to become a reality. It was something to do.

Shortly after we began to rehearse, John and I had our last fight. Rehearsals took on more meaning. Perhaps I could make a living for my baby and myself. Lila seemed pleased; she had always thought I had talent. My mother had always thought I showed artistic promise, but remarked, "You better get a job, nobody ever made a living singing folksongs."

The rest is my history and Lila's glory. As my picture, along with Peter's and Paul's, began to pop up in *Look* and *Life* magazines, Lila felt vindicated, because somehow I had pulled a rabbit out of the hat. She had known I was special and reminded her neighbors of all the cute things I'd done. Like any parent, she bragged.

Of all the awards for doing the work that has made me a success, Lila and William Turner's act of approval was the simplest and most moving. My picture joined the other "proud-ofs" on their wall.

They came to our first Carnegie Hall performance, Willie looking spiffy (but he always did like to dress nicely) and Lila, of course, looking like the mother of the bride.

The next several years passed quickly. Willie, who suffered from high blood pressure and diabetes, became ill and housebound. Lila asked me to get him a hospital bed, the kind that makes it easy to elevate your head or feet, and I did. Willie passed away in 1968. I was on the road.

Lila's great-grandchildren moved into her large apartment. She had raised three generations, and there would be four. It became my joy to help out. I sent her a small check every month and when she needed something, she had only to ask.

Her feeling about being helped was, and is, so different than my mother's. Lila felt it was a gesture of love and respect, something due. She never doubted that she had nurtured in good faith and deserved the same. My mother, on the other hand, looks at "help" as some sign of lost control over her own life. So I have to be very clever about offering.

Clearly one woman knew how and perhaps even when to ask. You can wait a long time for someone to "offer." There is a time when it is a greater gift to allow someone to give. Lila knew that. My mom's just beginning to.

In 1972, the end came sharply and too soon.

It's always "too soon" to lose a mother. On the road, I called Lila only to find out she was in the hospital. Stomach cancer is a swift killer. This was not something that would get better. It's funny how different people react to the potential loss of someone pivotal in their lives.

When you have time and you don't need a lot, you try to resolve the relationship while there is still life. It was that way with Lila and with my father. My father's death was much more complex. So much to resolve – guilt and anger over the loss of a whole relationship. But with Lila it was much more straightforward. I loved her, and she me, and there's not much more to say but thank you.

My first fur coat

I had bought my first fur coat that year, a mink. I could have bought one much sooner, but it wasn't the kind of thing you wear in a coffee shop or running around folk clubs in the Village. Somewhat shamefaced, I had finally bought one. I had done the obligatory rationalizations: it was practical, the eventual worn spots could be replaced, it was warm and in a cold hotel could be used as a blanket. But the real reason I bought it was it was as a symbol of success and of being grown up.

Grown-up New York women wore mink.

But Lila was dying, and I felt myself lose whatever handle on "grown-up" I had. My connection to my youth was in her memory. The stories she retold of mispronounced words, things I had said that were funny, all the confirmation that as a child, I had existed and been loved. She was dying. Her spirit, her humor, her belief that we would all survive whatever life dished out, that would be gone. I wanted her to live forever.

I stood at the door of my apartment wondering what to bring to the hospital. Flowers? A plant? She hated cut flowers. Then I remembered the story she liked to tease me about. That serious, condescending little girl who was going to give Lila all her old mink coats.

I went to the hospital to find Lila seemingly in control of the entire floor, putting on a pretty good show for a dying person. I spent the afternoon listening to her tell me "stories about Mary" for the last time. As I left, I took my coat and spread it over her lap. "There's the first of the old mink coats," I said as I left.

The service was held in a chapel not far from Lila's apartment. My mother went with me, she afraid that I would fall apart. My mother had always been afraid of strong emotions. But it was she who showed the most emotional stress. Suddenly, it became clear to me. As simple and direct as my relationship with Lila had been, hers had been complex.

Lila's presence had allowed my mother to work with a minimum of guilt, never an easy thing for working mothers. Lila had made work easier, but in the process, she became a strong rival to my mother for my affections. A battle I think my mother felt she had lost. But her gratitude to Lila far outweighed whatever resentment she had felt. Without Lila's strong hand, there were times when we all might have lost whatever sanity held us together as a family. Throughout both my mother's youth and my childhood, Lila had loved and nurtured us. My mother, as she wept, was being orphaned for the second time. As we held on to each other, I realized I would finally have to find a mother in my own.

Some of the faces in the chapel were familiar, and some I hadn't seen in years. Time had spun mother and me out to the edge of Lila's family orbit. We walked silently to the back of the chapel and sat down. A woman whom I later recognized as a neighbor of Lila's came over and whispered, "You should be sitting with the family." We did. I went up to the open casket to say goodbye. Her face was paler in death, her freckles more pronounced. Her Indian cheekbones and nose sharper. In life, Lila had been soft; in death, she looked determined.

The wake was held at "Uncle Willie's," her son's apartment. Culture defines the social place for grief. American blacks share with the Irish a sense that loss is personal, grief is communal. So it was that my daughter Erika and I went to the wake and found ourselves at a party.

Endless amounts of food. Fried chicken, potato salad, and cold cuts. Plenty of whiskey; a wake is not the place for beer or wine. And people, lots of people. Four generations of Lila's flesh. Decades of family and friends. People who had known me as a child, watched me grow up, and enjoyed my fame hugged and kissed and told my daughter stories about her mother, stories only they could tell.

Lola came over to where I was standing with her ex-husband in tow. The three of us laughed as Lola told of having to take me to the movies.

"God, how I hated that," she said. "You used to have a coat with a hood, and when I knew we'd have to take you to the movies with us, I'd push all that yellow hair in the hood and tell you to go out and play. I'd hope you got real dirty so nobody would notice." As she talked, I realized what she was really saying. Of course, taking a little girl on your date was bad enough, but a little white one must have been mortifying.

"You sure did cause some talk," she went on. "Poppa would be out on the stoop with his friends, and here you'd come up the Hill, screaming 'Poppa.' Caused a little talk in the neighborhood, I can tell you." "Or the times on the subway when you called him Poppa, and all the white people looking at him when you jumped into his lap. Well..." She let the rest of it hanging in the air. I got the message.

The past seemed to shimmer and come into focus, this time different. This time I saw it as an adult. I had thought of my childhood as easy, that these were people I had loved and who had loved me. It never occurred to me that I had ever been a problem, an embarrassment. But I had. How polite they had been, how generous. I had been a child.

Even in her death, Lila was still teaching me about love and respect. I didn't go to the cemetery. I couldn't. I wanted her to continue in my life, and the thought of watching her being locked into the ground was too final for me.

I drove to my house in Connecticut, stopping at a nursery to buy a small thin cherry tree. I cried as I planted it beside the house.

"Lila" is 20 feet tall now.

CHAPTER 2

Backstage

Singing: The Craft

Singing is a combination of two things — a natural sound, which is either pleasant or unpleasant, and a craft. One nature gives you, the other you develop. The craft of singing probably involves some very complicated physiology, but basically it's the ability to remember special relationships between one note and another and to reproduce them. Many people who can recognize when something is not in tune cannot sing on key. There's nothing wrong with their hearing. But there's something wrong with the way they've produced sound.

I've always felt that almost anybody could be taught to sing. Like any other kind of coordination, it's a matter of some discipline early enough in life. The problem is that many people are told they can't sing when they're young, so they give up. It isn't because they don't like music.

As my ears developed, I could hear I sang off-key, which I couldn't do in the beginning. As I began to hear it, it became painful to me. At this point in my life, it has become so painful that I have difficulty listening to some of my children sing. If we have the radio on in the car, the kids will be singing. One child, who shall remain nameless, sings incredibly off-key. It's like fingernails on the blackboard. I paid such a high emotional price for learning to sing on-key that I can't bear to hear anybody else sing flat or sharp. The image I have of singing on-key with a group is like swimming. When you have a good blend, you're cutting smoothly through the water. When you're off, it's like drowning or flailing.

Pitch was really a problem with PPM in the beginning. I sang flat. When Peter didn't sing with enough drive, he'd go under. And Paul consistently scooped or slid into notes. Paul was the foundation of the group, and it hurts when there's no foundation.

In fact, we were all singing flat most of the time. Milt Okun was sensitive enough not to tell us that directly, but I can remember him saying, "Think higher!"

You can get away with singing flat by yourself, but in a group it creates a cacophony. Certain dissonances are enough to send you to the booby hatch. Fortunately, I wasn't very aware of them in the early years, so they didn't bother me that much. They bothered Peter a lot.

Later, I sang much more accurately and Peter sang flat or sharp. I would soar into some three-part thing, and the mix would be so atrocious that I would stop singing. I just couldn't throw my voice into that mess, because it was so painful. And I suppose it must have been just as painful for him in the beginning.

The easiest way to see how we changed is to play *500 Miles* on our first album, then the *In Concert 500 Miles*, then *500 Miles* on the *All My Choices* album. Of course, by the time we did *In Concert*, we'd dropped a few notches in our range.

Singing must be very difficult for people who do not know how to put notes in the right places naturally. Singing is really a mental exercise, and if people learned it early enough, they could sing. I don't believe in tone-deafness. People are called tone-deaf when they can't reproduce sound. That's very different from being deaf to something. Tone-mute, maybe, but not tone-deaf.

Peter accompanies Mary on "500 Miles." (Photo by Robert Corwin/robertcorwin.com)

One of the things that corrected my pitch problems was singing in a group. You hear immediately when your voice is wrong because you're close to sounds you must mesh with, not grate against. It was fairly easy to tune myself up to match the other two voices or to find a place in between. That's a tremendous discipline, and I did it for years and years. I'm rarely off-key now, but I spent an awful lot of time listening and moving the note I was on up or down to make a pleasant sound.

Most people who sing alone don't have a corrective environment. Singing against a guitar never really gives you a mesh, since the sound of the guitar is not the same as the sound of the human voice. You have no basis of comparison. If you put two guitars together, you hear quickly enough if one is out of tune. You need two of the same kind of instruments to create an environment where you realize when you've got to move your note up or down.

I learned about singing through experience. I studied it as I studied everything else. I studied the things I liked. I never went to a teacher.

Once when I was having trouble with my voice, I went to a vocal coach. I was singing too high, which is very damaging. You can sing higher when you're not working your voice because your range is a good three or four notes higher then. Most amateur singers who sing in choruses are usually placed a little above where they can safely go. They couldn't sing there for a living. But as your voice matures, it drops. When mine dropped, I picked up notes on the bottom, so I stayed at the same number of octaves. As you work the voice, it begins to drop and find its meat.

A big part of my problem was singing too loud. It came from the effort to stay on pitch. The more volume I gave a note, the surer I could grab it. Also your psychic well-being has a direct bearing on the amount of energy you use to create a note. When you're very nervous, you tighten up your throat, your chest, and everything else. You begin to force the note through.

Singing well is like natural childbirth. In natural-childbirth classes, they teach you to lift up the muscles in your stomach. When you give birth, you have no control over the involuntary spasms of your uterus, but you do have control over the muscles that cover your uterus. If you're frightened, you have a tendency to tense those stomach muscles, and your uterus has to squeeze past the muscles that have flattened down on it. And that causes pain. If you can lift those muscles up and let the uteral contractions move freely, you have very little pain.

It's the same thing in singing. Many a node and polyp have been created by people who tensed up and forced the sound through their throats.

Imagine the inside of your throat as if it were a bird's back. You don't stroke a bird the wrong way. You'd break a lot of feathers. When you sing, you almost want to have the sound go through your throat without touching it. And it has to be very loose in there to do that. The moment you tighten your throat, you're already doing something you shouldn't be doing. Because volume doesn't have anything to do with your neck and throat. It has to do with your breath and how much force you put behind it.

I probably don't breathe correctly in terms of some kinds of vocal production. I don't have the breathing of an opera singer. But then I don't have to hold notes at volume levels that opera singers do. I don't have to breathe as correctly as they do.

I don't like trained voices. There is an unnaturalness about them. Opera singers are fabulous to watch, but they can only do what they've been taught to do. They're not very versatile. And they always have that over-trained, too-exquisite sound.

After pitch and breathing, the most important thing in singing is diction. There is nothing worse than not understanding what someone is singing. And if you're singing with a group, diction becomes especially important. Imagine the last word in a line you're singing appears to end in "ee." But it can be a long e, a short e, a fat e, or a thin e. If you take three voices, and nobody starts the "ee" in the same place or gives it the same value, you'll have something that sounds out of tune. So how you close on vowels is terribly important. You can drag that "ee" out or clip it off. And it's best to cut it off short. An "ee" sound is very difficult to keep in pitch.

One of the great joys in singing is sculpting sound. I remember once having to sing the word "peace" and wanting it to sound distinctly different from any other words in the sentence. The image in my head was that I wanted to sing the word so it would start to melt and be oozing but stay solid. I wanted the word "peace" to feel like peace of mind. I wanted to translate peace in a universal sense to a specific feeling of internal peace.

A writer deals with an entirely different kind of sound – what it sounds like when you don't say it. Anybody who's ever had to say an alliterative sentence loves it. Terrific to read, terrible to say.

So singing is like sculpting sound. A group that has a good blend is a group that sculpts the same way.

One of the most exciting things about PPM was the blend. And the nice thing about the blend was that it was composed of certain things that we agreed upon. Our arrangements were composed around our inadequacies. I think that made us more creative.

If you've ever tried to decorate an apartment in a new building, you know that it's impossible because it has no inadequacies that require creative solutions. If you move into an old building, it's loaded with inadequacies that often make you very creative. It's the same thing with making a meld in a trio.

None of us sat right in the middle of a true range. I'm not a soprano. I'm a mezzo-soprano, if anything. Peter is a tenor with baritone leanings. Paul is a baritone with bass leanings. So arrangements where Peter would take a line for half a stanza, I would take it for three notes, and he'd pick it up again. I could go where he couldn't go. People never realized that the leads were switching all the time. This made it interesting, and our arrangements had much more texture than if we'd been a perfect trio.

We had trouble sometimes making thirds. We used to have a part called the idiot part. Paul usually got it. The idiot part would fill up the holes. There's a melody line and a countermelody line above or below. The third part has to add little notes here and there that give the sound an interesting twist. A song can go along quite logically

34

and then make an idiot jump, a jump you'd never put in a melody or a countermelody. It will take an illogical jump up, then an illogical jump down. A melody flows. An idiot part has bumps in it. Except when you put it together, it sounds terrific. We used to call it the idiot part because it had no logic by itself. Very hard to remember. Stookey used to remember a lot of them.

When you move from the production of sound to recording it, you find other people sharing their particular crafts with you. We made our first album at a studio called Music Makers. The engineer was a guy called Bill Schwartau, who was a genius. Bill was Music Makers' best engineer, and he worked literally round the clock. A good engineer can work himself into the ground, and Bill did. He later had a terrible nervous breakdown and became an alcoholic. I'm sure that manic overwork started it. But he was brilliant, and he kept that studio alive.

You have a tremendous excitement when you first come to a recording studio and you realize what you're going to do. You don't know the medium, so everything seems exciting. Playbacks are especially exciting. And a studio has a reality of its own. It becomes a universe. It's like being in a time capsule. Time stops. Unless you happen to be paying for the session. Later on, time doesn't stop. But when you're new, you don't realize that the meter is running.

It was so exciting. And Bill was a marvelous person, very willing to teach you. We had experiments with different microphones to find the right one. We put them in different positions. Bill taught us about achieving dynamics with one another and how important it was. These were the days when you were dealing with only three tracks on a stereo record. Now people use 16, 22 even.

The reason for having more tracks is to have more control when you mix. Mixing allows you to determine the volume on each track. For instance, you may have horns, violins, guitars, and a piano, and after you've finished, you might decide that you didn't really like the violins. If the tracks are truly separate, if they don't leak onto each other, you can eliminate the violins by erasing them, or you can do what they call punch in – use only a certain part of the violin track. You have tremendous control.

And, in some ways, the mixing is as artistic as the artist himself. Many opera singers complain today because some tenor will be singing on a record with the same amount of presence as a bass. Sounds that are thinner and softer in live performances can be louder on a record. When you hear a record, you should hear what you'd hear if the artist were perfect. And today they have enough incredibly complicated equipment to almost make that happen.

At any rate, our first recordings were much simpler. Three tracks. Paul's guitar would be on the track with his voice. Peter's guitar would be on Peter's vocal track. And I was left with the bass. Which meant that a lot of the early PPM records did not have a solid bass sound to them because, if they had to turn me down, they had to turn the bass down as well. And they always had to turn me down. Mary always sang too loud.

Our first problem in recording was that Peter wanted perfection. That's a good thing to want, but we didn't have the equipment or know-how that you have now. Nowadays, you can record the instrumental track, get it perfect, and then lay your vocal tracks on top of it. It sounds as though you are singing with the band, but in reality you are singing with the band through earphones after the band has already been recorded.

In those days, you recorded directly with the band. If somebody made an instrumental mistake, you had to start all over, regardless of how wonderfully interpretive that particular vocal track was. I usually give my best performance on the fourth take. Peter and Paul's best instrumentals would usually be the 13th, 17th, or 18th take. By the time we got the band together, my pitch was very erratic and my voice was tired. When I get tired, I get snippy. My sense of humor is totally blown. And I used to have a very explosive temper. I think it was fear.

Those first sessions were laden with tremendous insecurity. If you blend insecurity with fear and fatigue, you have an explosive situation. The most classic was after a very grueling session where nothing seemed to go right. I finally turned to them and yelled, "Why can't you treat me like a fucking lady!" and stormed out. After everybody got over being stunned, they laughed a lot.

■

Although those first recording sessions were excruciatingly painful, the reason for much of the pain was that we cared very deeply about what the music sounded like. My biggest problem as a solo performer is trying to get a group of musicians to care the same way. They don't have the vested interest, and they don't have the enormous discipline that I've had. That Three Musketeers philosophy is missing. I go out on the stage with a band, and we're separate human beings. Living in separate worlds. I keep trying to figure out how to get them to think like one person.

At first, I thought, well, you just hire the best musicians. That's not the answer. The answer is to hire people who have a kind of naive enthusiasm, who like to play, who haven't reached the point of being jaded. Then you have a chance to think as one. Up till now, it's been my pulling in one direction and the band along for the ride. They're sure not part of the engine. And that's what I miss from Peter, Paul and Mary.

I remember when we got together again for a McGovern concert. It was terrific. Within four seconds, it was all there. That instinctive pull together. For all our yelling and crazies and hostilities, when we got on stage, we somehow managed to live for the sound we were going to make.

I think the Mills Brothers have it. I remember in Japan somebody said come hear the Mills Brothers. I thought he was kidding. Well, they're terrific. But they've spent their lives working together. Whether they speak to each other offstage or not, I don't know and don't care. When they're onstage together, they're a well-oiled humanity machine. Each one anticipates the other one. The dynamics are intuitive.

So caring is a big part of craft. And folksingers in particular used to have a total devotion to their art. Popular entertainment hadn't seen much of that before, and it probably won't again for a long time. It was a noncommercial quality. Popular performers always have to change their act to fit the going fad. But folk people became popular for what they were. We didn't change our thing to become popular. We were fortunate that it became a very big thing at a particular moment.

Look back at the Newport Folk Festival, for instance. The idea there was for professional entertainers to perform for nothing so that the public could see a Mississippi John Hurt, the Sea Island Singers from Georgia, some Canadian clog dancers, or a bunch of guys from a Texas prison. We all thought it was terrific, but it was unheard-of in any other branch of music. Jazz musicians never gave away anything.

We all did it though, and we all felt it appropriate that everyone should get union scale or get nothing. PPM was paid the same as the Georgia Sea Islanders.

I used to love to go to Newport. It was fun to hear all the ethnic music. We all felt an allegiance and a responsibility to the roots of what we were using. Every folk singer I knew, when he dealt with a traditional song, walked in gingerly. With care, with responsibility. You were dealing with something that was beautiful before you touched it, and you had a responsibility not to screw it up. Perhaps to interpret it your way, but not to kill it. It's a responsibility that pop singers don't have. A pop song is made for a moment, and if it survives that moment, terrific. If it doesn't, who cares? But folk music was music that had already survived.

It was like buying an antique. You don't put a fine antique in front of the radiator. When the Japanese bring ancient pieces of art to this country, they keep each piece in a glass case with a bowl of water inside the case to protect the piece from the dryness of American central heating. We felt the same way about a traditional song. You didn't take it out of context without the bowl of water.

I have tried to maintain that level of care in my own work. I try to be careful not only about the music but also about the lyrics of a song. In fact, I was trained to have battles with myself over lyrics.

As a soloist, I don't have the benefit of the two other editors I had with PPM. I have only my own editing. But sometimes I need a sounding board, and I sit down and work it out with my husband. We'll sit and talk about a verse until it's adjusted itself for me. I'll throw out an "F" or emphasize one word more than another. A change of emphasis is important because sometimes you can't change the words. You can call new writers on the phone and ask for a change, but you can't do that with certain established writers. Or if a song has been heard by a lot of people, they'll know it's changed and they'll want to know why.

It's especially good to talk the lyrics out if they have strong concepts. For instance, I did Graham Nash's "Southbound Train" on my third album. The lyrics were very appropriate politically for their time, which was after the McGovern defeat in 1972.

The last verse goes:

Fraternity, failing to fight back the tears
Will it take an eternity breaking the fears?
What will the passenger do when he hears
That he's already paid for the crown
On the southbound train going down.

For me, that was a very valuable kind of lyric — it said something to us embittered and griping Democrats who had paid for the crown.

It's hard to find songs like that — songs that have a social scope beyond personal experience. One can be corny about personal experiences. But when one talks about a social issue, the language must always go beyond trite symbols, which someone can discard quickly. You're not really trying to talk to yourself; you're trying to talk to somebody you haven't talked to before. Who doesn't agree with you? To do that, you have to rephrase the question in language that is not immediately recognizable. You have to avoid slogan language. You lose people right away if they can tie you to a slogan. If they can pigeonhole the song, they don't have to think about it.

One can become a better writer when one becomes a better editor. Editing is not a compromise. Editing is very difficult work. Some writers foolishly believe that if the words flow out naturally, they must be right. Some writers and some performers will not change their work because of fear and insecurity and pride. The idea that work must be right if it comes out naturally is bullshit. It can be right. It can also be wrong. It is certainly wrong in poetry and most other writing. Very rarely does anything come out in whole paragraphs. Editing is not a compromise. It is a compromise if an editor wants you to take a passage out of your book because he thinks you're wrong, or too esoteric, or too controversial. That's compromise.

But you have to know the difference between that and refining something, making it better and stronger. I remember watching somebody once making a little silver spoon. He started with a small bar of silver. And he explained that the more you pound the silver and heat it and then let it get cold, the more the molecules compress together. You end up with a tougher metal; it covers a larger area but is more tightly compacted. Good refining should do that – make something stronger and more beautiful. And that certainly isn't a compromise. You couldn't eat very well with a silver bar the shape of a Tootsie Roll.

A few final ideas about the craft of singing and performing involve live performances. Acoustics, for instance.

Amplified acoustics are always a problem everyplace. There's an unwritten law that says that if the natural acoustics of a hall are good, the electrified acoustics will be bad. If its electrified acoustics are good, its natural acoustics are bad. I don't understand sound. Nobody does, including the Bell Telephone Company. As we all remember from the saga of Avery Fisher Hall at Lincoln Center, you can spend millions of dollars on acoustics and get garbage. Some people say they understand, and some companies say they understand. But I know that they don't. It's an accident. And it's based on things that are unreal. If you have velvet seats and you decide to renovate the theater and change them to patent leather, you have just destroyed the acoustics of the room. Or if it's raining outside, and people come with damp clothes, the acoustics of the room will be slightly different that day. If it's a very rococo theater with lots of angels and cupids on the wall and somebody decides to clean it, you've changed the acoustics of the room.

Another important aspect of craft is knowledge of your own energy in a live performance. Nightclubs and concerts, for instance, demand very different approaches. You sing almost the same amount of time, but your adrenalin really gears you up and keeps you going for a concert. You get on the stage and you do two hours with a 15-minute intermission. Your energy level can easily sustain itself over a 15-minute break. But in a nightclub, an hour and a half between sets almost always means that your energy goes slack. It's like trying to play two basketball games with a lunch in between. That second one must be geared up on nerves.

It's hard to explain to non-performers that kind of energy used in performing. Sports are the best analogy. There's a deliberate physical drain that almost nothing else has. It's a total mental and physical involvement. So, for me, the second show in a nightclub is always inferior. You have to manufacture energy without having the buoyancy that comes from that first adrenalin flush. You're always a little nervous during the first set because it's new that night. But by the second set, you've been in the building so long and you've already conquered it once. You can't manufacture fear or the subtle set of things that pump up adrenalin. So it's like the second basketball game. You pull it out of your toes. I've had nights when I felt thousands of cells dying. Thousands of cells giving their life for that second show.

The Business

The music business is strange. In many ways, it's a very phony business. It involves some of the worst aspects of show business. A hit means a lot of money and a lot of wheeling and dealing. It gets very involved. A hit artist has to have accountants and lawyers and agents and record companies all over the world. And people are always trying to make a dollar. Some of them are not too honest. If the artist is sensitive at all, and most artists are to a certain degree, he has a tendency to shrink from it and say you to take care of it.

I can understand how artists end up with no money after tremendously successful careers. And it's interesting that it happens to women so often. Women seem programmed to turn their affairs over to men, and many of the men in the music business are really unscrupulous when it comes to dealing with women.

Managers, agents, lawyers have hostile attitudes toward artists. Most of them think that the artists are ding-dongs. They may be able to manufacture all that money out of some weird talent, but they don't understand anything. Well, of course, artists don't have degrees in business administration. They're not accountants. Further, most managers don't want to teach you anything about the business. If they did, what the hell would you need a manager for? So they're not very quick to explain anything. And many artists – me included – have a tendency not to listen even when people do explain things to them.

Having a contract explained to me made me feel like a kid in school. It was like learning something unpleasant that I really didn't want to know about. I think many artists have a childish desire to be protected and taken care of. The burden of doing your artist's work makes you feel that you shouldn't have any other obligations. It's a disastrous indulgence. A lot of people who made millions of dollars for other people are out on the street without two cents in their jeans. Taking care of business is a talent. You have to pay attention.

I sometimes feel ashamed that I know as little as I do about the business. I've spent the last several years trying to rectify that. Artists have a tendency to sign anything put in front of them. Your accountant tells you we just borrowed $50,000 from the bank. Your natural reaction is to ask why. Well, he says, we're paying taxes this way and blah blah blah – a 20-minute spiel. And you figure they know. Part of my Puritan background says I don't want to owe the bank anything, but you sign.

What disturbs me most is the deliberateness of the artist who says, "I don't want to know." It's really childish. But success and power frighten artists. Nobody feels justified about having the kind of power that the successful artist has. As success begins to blow you more out of proportion, transferring power over your life to your business associates may be a psychological attempt to make yourself more life-sized.

There are some exceptions. Rod McKuen is a very good businessman. So is Harry Nilsson. Katherine Hepburn is exceptional in this – as in nearly everything. She said on the Dick Cavett show that she never had an agent. She negotiated all her contracts herself, and her father took care of her money and gave her an allowance until he died in 1962. She was always the first lady against the world. But these are the few artists I know of who are capable of handling their own affairs. Most performers are the worst.

A major aspect of fame is the enormous amount of money you begin to make. Most people who get hit with the first flash of money start to live out their fantasies. For some it's cars; for others it's clothes or a new house. Some people, I suppose, are born conservatives and probably stash away every penny. When I didn't have any money, I always thought money was an abstraction with relatively little meaning. When I had it, I spent it; when I didn't, I didn't. I didn't make myself crazy because I didn't have it. If I had $50 in my pocket and I saw a $40 sweater in the window, I bought it. If I had $5 in my pocket, I said to myself, "Better get a job."

As a result, when I got a lot of money, I was ridiculous with it. I opened a charge account at Bendel's and bought a lot of clothes, some of which were silly. My worst mistake was a $1,000 evening dress that I wore once. That was my biggest single mistake, but I made a lot of little ones that probably added up to more. I think my major mistake in the beginning was that I bought clothes that were too old for me. I was developing something called taste, and since I'd always thought my mother was well-dressed, I ended up buying things that looked terrific on my mother. Elegant, matronly, Pauline Trigère.

All three of us threw a hell of a lot of money around. Some of it was well-thrown. A lot of it was dumbly thrown. Peter and I both threw a lot of money away on artworks, but that's not throwing it away. I don't plan to sell my paintings, but that money is fundamentally retrievable. Paul had a solid Midwest upbringing that said, "Own your own house." So he owned a lot of houses. Bought one for his folks, one for himself. Money doesn't breed taste, but it does have a tendency to make acquirers out of people. The newly rich have a greater tendency to experiment with art. They've traditionally gotten in on the ground floor with new artists, and in doing so, ended up in their old age with Monets and Modiglianis. The nouveau riche of the Forties have some good art collections. But there are all kinds of taste. Nouveau riche homosexual is usually exquisite. But it's too busy for my taste. Little collections of things lying about. Cloisonné boxes all over. Agate eggs.

I never understood the concept of old money. I think people with old money have a tendency to lose their sense of adventure. I don't plan to leave my children a lot of money. If I'm 99, they better put me in an institution, because if I see that I've got $20 in the bank, I'll spend it.

I've set up trust funds for my children to get through college, but I plan to spend every other penny myself. If they like to live high, they'll have to figure out a way to do it on their own. I'm not about to make them leeches on life. I didn't have them to do that with them.

I've never really examined what untold wealth would do to me. I think my first impulse would be to buy a lot of houses. I'd live part of the year in London, part of the year in the south of France, and part of the year in Connecticut. My second impulse would be to realize that I have already acted out that fantasy – almost. I own a house in Connecticut that I love. And you can only look at one garden a season. I almost bought a house in the south of France once, but the thought of it made me feel disloyal to the poor little house in Connecticut. A vegetable garden in the south of France is no improvement over a vegetable garden in Connecticut.

You have to be trained to spend money wisely. Either you train yourself, or somebody else trains you. But it's inevitable that anyone who comes into a lot of money quickly spends like a drunken sailor. The question is whether or not you get over it.

It's a question of management. A lot of managers could really save their clients a great deal of money if they put them on allowances. But it's very hard to take somebody who has some independence and tell him how much he'll spend. Also, I think managers enjoy the reflected glory of their clients' conspicuous consumption. They like to send clients around in limousines they can't afford. It makes the manager look more successful.

Management is an enormous question. In my career with PPM, I never felt I knew what was happening. It was like being kept. We had an accountant, lawyers, a manager, all of whom took care of everything. I never knew how much money we made. If we did a concert and our fee was $15,000, I never knew how much of that $15,000 I would ever see. The agent's fee, the management fee, the cost of shipping the band and the sound equipment – that all came out first. By the time the dollar got down to me, it wasn't anywhere near $15,000. But I never knew what it was. I never thought of a concert as being a personal net to me of a thousand dollars or whatever.

I never knew, and I never knew for several reasons. One, I never asked. And I didn't ask for complex reasons. If I didn't ask, I thought it would just keep coming. I didn't want to be a grown up in that situation. I didn't want to be responsible or worry about money. I'm sure I made it very easy for everyone else to run the business. I just assumed that my manager would do the right thing, the accountant would do the right thing, and the lawyers would do the right thing. It never occurred to me that they all had a vested interest. It's occurred to me since.

What management did in those days was fascinating. I say in those days because I think the role of management is changing. Some very interesting business changes have occurred in the show-business world. In the old days, your manager took anywhere from 10 to 25 to 50 percent depending on how dumb you were, and the agency got ten percent for booking agents. Lawyers used to be paid by the hour. So were accountants. Then accountants began to be paid by the year or on a retainer. And lawyers began to be paid on retainer. And now lawyers are asking for a percentage of your income. So are many accountants. That puts them smack in the middle of management, but without any of the problems of management.

The concept of what a lawyer's services really include has changed. I think all those lawyers got tired of making big record contracts for artists and, after they'd negotiated the contract, watching the manager skim off a percentage. A lot of lawyers have a lot of chutzpah. But they shouldn't get paid like management unless they're going to work like management. And if they are, then you don't need a manager. I wish they'd make up their minds about what they are. Unfortunately, the best lawyers are specialists. If you hire a lawyer who's a specialist in the music business, it's worth a great deal to you that your contract be right. On the other hand, what do you need a manager for? A manager used to be the specialist.

A manager, as I understood it when I began in the music business, was a person who had a tremendous range of contacts. He was supposed to be able to negotiate for you in television, radio, movies, record company contracts, and almost anything else. He was also supposed to have in the back of his head a master plan to launch you into success. For this, you paid him a percentage of your income. It seemed fair enough, since he was the person who was going to make you have an income.

A manager was the person who picked your agent. He shopped around. He would know the scuttlebutt about who was a good agent for what. He'd negotiate your contract with your agent. The agent, in turn, got you performing jobs. He would contact the schools, work out the individual contracts with each employer, try to route your road tours so they made some kind of sense. The agent would be the person to talk to television people and get you a spot on a television show. He would tell your manager when he felt your price could go up. He was the guy who understood what the traffic would bear and where the traffic was.

Your lawyer did your wills, what personal business you had, helped you form a publishing company, incorporated you. He negotiated your record contracts. And his expertise could make a lot of money for you. Your manager hired him.

So the manager was someone whose authority could easily be encroached upon. But your manager never let you know it. You never heard from him how important the lawyer's role or the agent's roles were. He hired them. He was the executor of your estate, real or imagined. He had the final authority. But managers were supposed to be something else, too.

They were supposed to guide your career. They were supposed to have a point of view that would be impossible for you to have because of your involvement. They were supposed to protect you from the ups and downs. Artists run on a lot of ego and need a tremendous amount of encouragement. Almost everybody else does, too, but artists have always said it out loud. Everybody understands that artists need a lot of encouragement.

A manager was the buffer between you and the real world. If the record company was unhappy with you, he didn't tell you. Most artists prefer to live in blissful ignorance of those things. We deal with it very snobbily; we pretend we shouldn't be concerned with mundane commerce. But I still think the greatest fear most performers have is the fear of bouncing a check.

A manager was a father figure, someone who would take you aside and say, "Listen, you can't do this," or "You gotta do that." He'd come to the shows. He was supposed to look at what you were doing and give you advice about it. He was able to give you an outside look at yourself. Perspective. I always felt that managers had a tremendous position of control that most of them didn't exercise. As long as PPM was making money, we could do anything we wanted to do. And I don't think our manager was alone in this. I'm sure the Beatles' manager faced the same problem. Nobody tried to control an artist's personal behavior if he was making money.

Some managers will allow their artists to cancel concerts. Now that is bad. It makes producers wary of you. It's expensive. Yet many performers do it at the drop of a hat. They do it because they can get away with it. Or so they think. They do get away with it with the authority figures who are close to them. But they don't get away with it with the public. Sooner or later the public says, "Oh, you never know whether so-and-so is going to show up." By then, it's too late.

Managers are not well known for disciplining the emotional excesses of their clients. Every business has certain rules and it would help performers to know what they are early in the game. If you show up late to a gig, if you don't show up at all, if you cancel, if you fool around with kids who are underage, there are ramifications. So there are some very simple rules. And they apply just as well to the trucking business as to show business. Because the results are the same. If you can't be counted on to deliver the goods, you won't be hired.

One of the problems of quick success is that it tends to give people an unreal sense of power. And it is unreal. The public may give you a lot of power, but they'll take it away from you just as fast as they gave it to you. Twenty-five years ago when Ingrid Bergman had a child out of wedlock, the public shut her down. On the other hand, Katherine Hepburn was having an affair with a married man, Spencer Tracy, for all those years and the world didn't shut her down. She played by a certain sense of rules. She didn't flaunt it. Therefore, the world let her get away with it.

Sooner or later, somebody else's morality or economics will affect you. You can get an audience so excited that it tears up a theater. The audience may not shut you down, but the theater owner will.

It always seemed to me that managers failed when they went along for the ride as long as you were making money. They could never use the ultimate threat then. They could never say, "Have somebody else manage you."

If you're dealing with a 20-year-old performer who doesn't know diddly-squat, he's controllable to a certain extent. You can pound the rules into his head before he's a success. Break the rules and there will be repercussions. But if you allow a performer to become an anarchist, you'll never get any control back. But managers don't seem to care about that. They want the money, but they don't want the responsibility.

The temptations to indulge oneself are all there. Everybody's willing to give you anything. A 25-year-old guy hits it big, and everything he could possibly want is available. He's got the money to buy the best motorcycle in the world. He can buy an airplane. Thousands of young girls crowd him at every concert, and some offer him their frames. They'll pick up and travel with him. Drugs, booze, anything he wants, it's all there. It's a very self-centered time. He walks into a room and everybody does whatever he wants to do. When he leaves, the retinue leaves with him. It's tremendous power. And in the name of artistic "I'll do whatever I want," he'll waste thousands and thousands of dollars making albums that have no business being made. Or he'll delay making any albums at all. Once he finds that someone will hold a plane for him, he'll never be on time for a plane again. All the petty neuroses then become "virtues."

It's very important for the artist to have certain external disciplines, which may seem to be commercial and arbitrary and dumb but that are the only things that make an artist finish something. Indecisiveness in art can be deadly. I'm very happy, in retrospect, that we had deadlines. If we hadn't, we would never have completed much. Record companies insist on deadlines. If they didn't, they'd never receive any product. And the artist would never have any exposure.

A manager with a young act can help an artist learn discipline. I don't mean that a manager is supposed to be a perpetual father, and I don't think that all artists are children. But many start out as children, and I've often felt that many managers, because of greed, allowed their clients to be destructive in both business and human terms. They were afraid to say no. And having never said no, they were in no position to start.

■

PPM's manager, Albert Grossman, has always been a mystery to me. Albert was either very brilliant or very lucky. He did go through a string of incredible successes – PPM, Bob Dylan, Janis Joplin, and a few others. That's big.

When I first met Albert, I had already heard about him. He had a reputation as a folk entrepreneur. Albert was from Chicago, and he had opened a club there called the Gate of Horn. The folk scene in those days traveled from city to city. For a while, New York was the center of things, and then it was Chicago, then San Francisco, then Los Angeles.

The folk scene had a tendency to ripen in a city, produce whatever that area had to offer, and then move on. Very few folk clubs were around in the early and mid-Fifties. The Gate of Horn was one, and the hungry i in San Francisco was another. New York was fairly barren, but Boston had Club 97. Little folk pockets were here and there.

Albert discovered a banjo player and singer named Bob Gibson, who was not to be believed. He played the most incredible banjo. I met him and he was charming. Needless to say, I fell madly in love with him, as did probably half the ladies who saw him. He was a ladies' man, too, on top of it all. And Albert was his manager.

Albert also managed Odetta, who was an enormous name in the folk world at that time. The folk world was small and ingrown then, but it had its stars. They weren't stars in popular acclaim like Harry Belafonte, who really wasn't a part of the folk scene. Folk stardom was clique stardom. I'm sure all the saddle makers in America know each other and know who's the best. Well, Odetta and Bobby Gibson were the best in folk music. And Albert handled both of them. I would hear his name bandied about, and I once met him at a party with Odetta. He was a round-faced and rather large man. He always had a mass of gray hair.

I must have made some kind of impression on Albert; otherwise, he wouldn't have said to Peter, "She's a good singer if you can get her to work."

So I really met Albert when he introduced me to Peter with the idea of auditioning for him. Albert came to the apartment – the one that was four-and-a-half inches wide and had all the cockroaches. It was quite a scene. Albert had a mystery about him. He was the big gun. The magic man. I'm sure I never would have done it if Albert hadn't said, "Let's get the group together."

Albert grew his hair halfway down his back and wore a ponytail and little Ben Franklin glasses. People used to describe him as looking like Martha Washington. He went through a period where he wore nothing but collarless Mexican peasant shirts, and he was always popping a button. The "Smilin' Jack" comic strip had a character who was fat and was always popping buttons, and a chicken followed him around eating the buttons. That image used to come to mind with Albert. His disarray was always the wrong kind of disarray. In later years he'd be sitting in his Silver Cloud Rolls Royce, his hair would be tied back with an icky rubber band, and his Mexican shirts would be popping their buttons at his stomach. He was like a grown-up teddy bear.

A very interesting mixture, Albert. He was a connoisseur of art and other expensive things. When we were working, he would spend – without turning a hair – $5,000 on a chair. But he never spent anything on his appearance. In the beginning, I used to feel, well, that was his thing. But as we got older and richer, I realized that it was a kind of affectation that didn't make sense to me.

At any rate, I really didn't have a lot of contact with Albert. We auditioned for him. Then we had contracts and business meetings, but he and I didn't see much of one another. He was Peter's manager originally, and I think because he came to us in that position he aided and abetted Peter in being the leader. PPM was lucky because we were the first of Albert's clients who made it in a big commercial way, and we got the benefit of stable business associates. We got Tom and Ed Sarkesian, for instance, our concert producers. We got a decent law firm. We got a good accountant.

Peter thought the sun rose and set on Albert. He still does. That's what kept the relationship afloat so long. It became sticky at some points, because I was not always that happy with Albert.

Albert had great power – still. The value the music business places on some people amazes me. Albert has a great deal of power at Warner Brothers, for instance. The artists who actually make the money have very little power. If I called up Joe Smith tomorrow and said I heard a terrific singer, he'd say ho-hum. If Albert called him up and said he heard a terrific singer, he'd say I'd love to hear him. It amazes me and sometimes makes me smile, because it's the way empires rise and fall. The people in power always begin to trust themselves. They trust only the executors of the estate and never look at the estate. And the estate is what will continue.

It's happening in the country. The politicians have forgotten what America is, and they are only trusting the executors of the estate. So it's a bunch of lawyers talking to each other. It's the same thing with those managers. Warner Brothers is going to take the biggest bath ultimately because it doesn't trust the artist. It doesn't understand the artist or trust the artist; it trusts only the managers of the artists.

The Artist

How are performers different from other people? Anybody in the arts has a tremendous desire to spit out something he feels. Some of them spit it out because they need to be heard. Others spit it out for fear that it will overcome them if it stays in. I think the reason for spitting it out makes the difference between one kind of performer and another. But they all come to the same place, where spitting it out is a release. It's what keeps them sane or in balance with themselves.

And what they get for the spitting out is an immediate pat on the head. Not a delayed one. A lot of people say that performers are immature. Someone once told me that a sign of maturity was the ability to delay gratification. You're too busy to go to the movies today, but you can go tomorrow. "OK," says the mature person. The immature person says, "I have to go now." A performer does his work and is instantly gratified – even if he's not particularly successful. Performers are rarely booed off the stage. You can be awful and still get a round of applause.

So the performer gets gratification immediately. And he knows exactly where he can get it again. Writers and painters are lonelier in that respect. They get a gratification from doing. They get their own pat on the head when they finish the chapter.

The artist has a special advantage in that he has no middleman. A lot of middlemen sell his product, but they don't make it. It's just you. You write the book or you don't write the book. You paint the picture or you don't paint the picture. You sing the song or you don't sing the song. Nobody comes and helps you on Tuesdays. Yes, there's machinery to deal with – agents and managers and whatnot. But when you get on the stage, nobody can open your mouth for you.

That gives you a tremendous sense of knowing who you are. You don't always think you're a good artist. You can doubt whether you're saying anything profound or not. But you know that you're not just anybody. There definitely is a difference. A girl at a switchboard is one of thousands and has more in common with more people than she would like to have. I'm not in common with anybody. I've spent a lifetime being different. Not in profound ways. I have a husband, I have children, I have a house. I get bored and look up something different in a cookbook. In that way, I'm no different from millions of women. But I'm different in that I know how to do something that is different. Nobody else sounds quite the way I do. Being any kind of an artist does give you a sense of your uniqueness. And that's worth a lot to a lot of people.

A sense of uniqueness can sometimes mean a sense of being alive. When I drop dead, *The New York Times* will have an obit. That switchboard operator won't. When I move through life, I make ripples. Not necessarily massive ones, but ripples.

Oddly enough, artists have a tendency to believe that we're freer than other people. We're not really. We have a freedom that's defined by society, and it's no freer than anybody else's. I know that if I don't perform, I'm trapped. So although performing gave me an identity, I have to support it.

A lot of subtleties can complicate your freedom. Whose creation are you really? Are you Mary of PPM, or are you Mary Travers the performer, or are you Mary yourself? Which one of those folks are you?

Still, you have a lot of power. I can talk about anything, and people will listen. They can reject me if I don't make sense, but I can make them listen. The artist can create feelings that an audience will share and recognize. That's his talent. But I don't understand why one person can do it and another can't.

I go and look at Monet's "Water Lilies," and it never fails to move me. And I know that the reality wouldn't move me as much. I could walk up to a pond full of water lilies and say, "Breathtaking, beautiful. Let's go eat." The painting evokes other things. Art makes you see and feel more than surface reality. You can live with someone and never find in that person the depth you might see in a portrait or a character in a novel.

What makes performers different is that they see differently. I don't think they always know they see differently. I don't think Billie Holiday ever intellectualized how she saw. It was a gift. They see, and their lives are not necessarily better for the seeing.

An artist often has insights that he doesn't understand. I think anyone who's ever written a poem has written lines or used images for which he has no explanation. He can read it years later and see a vision of himself that he didn't understand at that time. I once wrote something about being pregnant with Erika and about my relationship with my husband at the time. I was feeling lonely and quizzical about birth. When I read it years later, I realized that emotionally I knew exactly what was happening to my marriage, exactly what my complaints were. I felt it and wrote it, but no bell rang in my head and said, "If you feel it, understand it."

The performer can hit the nail on the head like that all the time and still wreck his life again and again. The connection between his emotional life and his intellectual life is missing. The link isn't necessary for the performer, as a performer. Sometimes the person who's unable to make the hookup is more driven to spit his emotion out.

The level of ego also makes performers different. I mean ego in the sense of who am I to presume that I have the right to say anything. We have a need to override our own insecurity about whether we have the right to say anything. That need is ever-present. We have a need, and we've found a place to satisfy it. That makes us different. But it doesn't eliminate the need. It doesn't give you peace of mind. You still need to express yourself.

All performers are somewhat lonely. They suffer from an intense relationship with themselves. They're quite selfish, but not in the greedy sense. It's a self-absorption. Their focus is doing something personally. They spend their lives constructing situations to make that easier for them. They themselves are central, and they have a special awareness of their centralness. Most other people give up their centralness to a family, a marriage, a job. When you develop a central feeling about yourself, you tend to group other people into helpers or enemies. Nobody can share your feelings with you, no matter how much they love you or want to help you. You end up having to do it by yourself. It isn't like building a house where you can call in the neighbors to help you paint.

Your needs will be met only if you meet them. So it's not surprising that most artists are solo workers. And that too makes it a problem to hold a group together. Collaboration is a strain. It must be terrifying for a person like Bernie Taupin, a songwriter who works with Elton John and some other talented performers. By himself, unless he develops a talent for writing books or something, he'll always need a musician.

Artists are aware of being different. It comes from feeling alone, but I don't know which comes first.

I suspect feeling alone comes before creativity. I think loneliness is the root of certain kinds of creativity. Most artists need introspection. Whether it's thought out or felt out, it has to be there. And usually the only people with time for introspection are people who feel alone, who are not caught in the rush of companionship. I never liked the notion that all artists had unhappy childhoods, or that they were neurotic, but the myth has a certain truth. I think they felt different and not quite connected. Because part of the search in art is to connect. If you feel connected, you don't go looking for connections.

Each performer reaches out for connections in his own way. Some performers can get an audience to sing and some just can't. Some performers get on stage and reveal a twisted self-sorrow. They ask you to watch it, to identify with it, but you have the safety of knowing that it's their sorrow, not yours. Other performers, especially comedians, are everyman. A comedian can get an audience to do a lot of things because he bases his communication on the sameness of people. He understands you and you understand him. You don't, as an audience, necessarily understand Joni Mitchell. You're invited to be a voyeur of sorts.

The performer who makes you feel that the only difference between you and him is that he can sing or string words together is someone you'll sing along with. I don't think, for example, that Beethoven could have gotten us all to sing. Well, the Ninth, maybe. Pete Seeger, on the other hand, is your uncle. He shares with you. He and the audience become one. But some performers start out with the premise that they are greatly different from the audience. They build their success on the idea of a difference.

Compare the success of a Judy Garland with the success of a Bing Crosby. He related to everybody. He wasn't too good-looking, no tremendous power. Soft and easy. Judy Garland was dealing with a lot of torture. Her most loyal fans were people who identified with that torture. She had a large homosexual audience, people who knew they were tortured and alone. They related to a woman who tried to commit suicide any number of times, who was a drunk, who was leading a miserable life.

Each artist has an audience. Bubble-gummers, rock 'n' rollers, acidheads, homosexuals, mass America. And when an artist becomes middle of the road, he's relating to a large, stable cross-section of people.

David Buskin. David's success will be decided by timing. If he had begun writing and singing just before Bob Dylan, he'd be a giant today. An immense success. But right now, people aren't recognizing literacy. We've sunk into wordless rock. And David needs a literate audience. Now take a John Denver, he's easy. You soak him up like a sponge. That's not to put him down. But he's optimistic and accessible and uncomplicated.

A lot of people think that artists change with fame. They don't change fundamentally. But the strongest force in their life expands. Fame allows people who are afraid to be shits to become shits. It lets the closet shit come out into the open. But it doesn't mean he wasn't

Peter, Paul and Mary reunited on stage. (Photo by Robert Corwin /robertcorwin.com)

a shit all along. It's just that he was scared somebody would punch him. The people who are nice but shy get nicer. Many people who are basically self-destructive never learn that fame doesn't relieve whatever made them self-destructive to begin with. Fame may accent it. It may make them feel more alone. But it only expands a basic tendency.

I think I've been self-destructive in my life, but never bottom-line self-destructive. I've never entertained thoughts of suicide or thought it was all over. I've been down, but I always knew I was going to get up. It was just a question of when. By the same token, I've never entertained great flights of fancy about huge success. I was always very insecure about success. When I sang a song well, I preferred to praise the song, not the singer. I'd say it was a good song. It became a family joke. I was ready to dump the praise someplace else because if you accept the responsibility for having done something well, it means you have to live up to it. So, for a long time, in my own particular neurotic state, I preferred to think that success was an accident.

But I don't think that that fame and fortune are dangerous. Except for very young people. I was 23 when it hit me, which I don't think is very young, although it seems younger to me all the time. I was an old 23. If your values are elastic enough to change and grow, you can take a lot of fame without falling apart. If your values are not developed, then sudden fame will blow things out of proportion.

I never thought that fancy people were worth more or were more important to know. I know this world has its stars, but when I thought about them as human beings, I knew they went to the bathroom, too. Very few people have struck awe into me. There are people who inspire awe, like Katherine Hepburn, but very few human beings have awed me. Some have pleased me or made me proud. By the same token, I've never felt that Mary of PPM was entitled to anything extra. People who have given me something extra for being a performer have always embarrassed me. That's not to say that I haven't used that extra edge on occasion. I've been glad that someone gave it to me. But I've known that he or she was full of shit, and I was too.

I remember once wanting to see a movie that had an incredible long line. My secretary said, "Well, I'll call the theater, and they'll let you in." I was embarrassed, but I let her do it. I would never have called myself. The worst temptation is when someone offers to do something for you that you'd be embarrassed to do for yourself.

Fame is a game, and a lot of people play it. Some restaurants will give you first-class-plus treatment for the same money because you're different. Some people love to run that number in restaurants. Peter used to. It made me crazy. I go to a restaurant to eat. If I go to a very good restaurant and I pay that bloody check, the service better be good. But it should be good for anybody who's going to pay the check – whether you're a UN diplomat, a performer, or a visiting fireman.

I think one of the terrible things about show business fame is that you face a lot of stuff you don't understand. If a man succeeds in business, he understands how he succeeded. He usually learns at a steady rate so that when he gets to the top, he knows in very specific terms what he did and what it cost. In show business, more often than not, success hits very quickly. You may have been in the business a long time, but the jump between obscurity and fame is a big, quick one. It's hard to understand what happened. It seems silly that one song should be so different from the rest of the songs that you've picked to sing. But one good hit single can catapult somebody from the minor leagues to the majors in a period of six weeks. All of a sudden, someone who was working for $1,500 a night is making six, seven, eight, nine thousand.

But you don't know how to keep your earnings up there, because your business isn't like other businesses. A performer can make peanuts one year, a million the next, and peanuts the year after. He may never know why or how everything went up or down. The artist's life is precarious, and the idea of sustaining success is maybe the biggest problem of all. It may be even more difficult than getting success.

Individual songs become hits for strange, existential reasons and they last only for a moment. A moment is not a sustaining career.

Somebody who can sell a lot of albums consistently, without hit singles, is an artist who has become an institution, but usually the question of growth in show business is very sad. We live in a disposable society, and we don't allow our performers to grow. So-and-so was a hit yesterday, but somebody is always available to fill that position tomorrow. A performer can have the wisdom to say, "I'm only going to do one album a year, and I'm only going to do 25 concerts a year, because I am a singer and a writer, too, and I have to have time to write." But then he can pass out of existence by not being on the scene.

Show business has no middle class. Once you've reached the top, the only other place to go is the bottom. It's especially hard for singers. An actor plays many different characters and each new character can be a new challenge. But a singer is in a rut. Song to song, you play yourself. You are your style.

Music audiences fall in love with a style. They don't fall in love with you or with your content. Sooner or later, they will discard the style, just as they have discarded other styles. Some singers survive it. But they have to be bloody brilliant. At least in the pop-music world. So singing, like most of the arts, has its cruel and difficult side. Success and failure are agonizingly visible.

A Sad Note at the End of the Song

(Bucks County Courier Times)

SEPTEMBER 24, 1987

The best part of a Peter, Paul and Mary concert for me is when the audience sings along. They sing because they know the words and the music is part of all our pasts.

After 26 years, there's a lot of continuity between us and our audiences. Often there are three generations, all of whom have shared our music with their families. But the job of being a performer has duties I never could have anticipated.

When performers are on stage in front of thousands of people, they are in charge of communication. The job we signed on for was to communicate a series of ideas encompassed in the music. And it's a job I have loved for these 26 years. Occasionally, because we are the ones with the microphone, we're asked to make announcements, such as notifying a person in the audience that his car is blocking another or has its lights on.

Once, when the smell of gas pervaded an auditorium where we were singing, we had to advise the audience to make an orderly exit and stay on stage until they had done so. Our job was panic control that night.

This month, we were handed the hardest job of all.

Peter, Paul and Mary was singing in Minneapolis at the State Fair. During the intermission, a fair official asked us to request that a woman come backstage. Her husband had been killed in a light plane crash and she had to be notified.

The fair's representative was sensitive and requested that we delay the announcement until they could locate a chaplain. They didn't want her to be notified just by a policeman.

So the three of us went backstage with the terrible knowledge that somewhere out there a woman was about to have her life shattered. And that we would be the ones to begin the most terrible day in her life.

The act of singing takes concentration and focus. And we were fighting the distraction of the information we held. In a very real sense that woman's life remained stable and secure for as long as we kept singing.

It felt almost vulgar to be the stranger who knew something so personal about her life when she did not.

It was hard to face the fact that we were making the audience laugh and sing, including her, for we were caught between a crushing sadness for an unknown woman and an anger that we had been made the messengers of the worst possible kind of news.

As we came to the end of the concert, Peter asked the woman to come backstage. Deliberately, he put the request among some other public announcements, hoping she and others would think her car had been improperly parked.

The chaplain was waiting. He requested that we keep her company until the squad car to take her home was brought backstage.

Each in turn, we held her. Her name is Cathy, and she is our age, with two children, one 21 and one 18.

She and her husband had gone to college listening to Peter, Paul and Mary. We had been a part of the beginning of their adult lives. They had loved and laughed with us and shared our music with their children. We had been a part of their lives together.

Now we were a part of its end. And so we cried together.

Glamour Is in the Eye of the Beholder
(Bucks County Courier Times)

May 26, 1988

The other day in the Chicago airport, a woman who recognized me told me how lucky I was to be in such a glamorous job with all that travel to exciting places.

Having gone to bed at 1 a.m. and gotten up at 6 to be in the lobby at 7 to get to the airport by 8 to catch a 9 o'clock flight, I wasn't feeling so lucky as just downright sleepy. In show business one must get to the airport an hour before flight time because you must not miss the flight when you are doing one-nighters. Neither must your luggage.

We'd look silly arriving on stage without two guitars and a bass.

If you think the airlines like that bass, think again. It's a classical upright. In its case it must weigh 125 pounds. It's large, unwieldy and takes two people to carry it on and off the plane.

Now it flies in the hold. In the old days it used to sit in its own seat. If you suspected that the seats in airplanes are getting smaller and closer together, you're right.

The nice lady sitting next to me was a bit nervous about flying, so she chatted away.

"You must have been simply everywhere, seen so many cities," she exclaimed.

I have and I haven't. I've been to every major and a few minor cities in the country, but I wouldn't go so far as to say I've seen them. I have seen the airports, the highway to the hotel, the hotel, the theater, and its reverse route. All in a 24-hour period.

That's not seeing America. Sometimes I feel like I'm living the movie, "If It's Tuesday This Must Be Belgium."

Take the last two weeks: Wednesday, Fort Worth; Thursday, Tulsa; Friday, San Antonio; Saturday, Orlando; Sunday, Ft. Lauderdale; Monday fly back to New York; Thursday, Stamford for two whole days; Saturday, Dayton; Sunday, Cincinnati; Monday, fly back to New York. Sound like fun?

The last two weeks of July and all of August are even better with 26 concerts in six weeks. That's 26 different cities.

A typical day for me is one of perpetual motion. Here's the itinerary for just one day:

Depart airport 9:10 a.m.; arrive Dallas 11:49; drive to hotel, arrive and check in 1 p.m.; eat, mini-nap, call home and then go to theater for sound check at 5; rehearse at 6; change and makeup; performance at 8 until 10:30; change and sign autographs; leave theatre at 11:30; back to hotel at midnight. Sleep until 8 a.m. and repeat for four consecutive days with slight variations.

When I was younger, 25 years ago, this was fun. Now, although my throat thinks it's still in its 20s, my feet know they're 51. Airport gates get farther and farther from the main terminal, stages seem to get harder. Airplane food is more like cardboard.

So why do I do it?

The pay is good, the audiences are wonderful, and I still love singing.

"Do you love being recognized and having to sign autographs?" She flowed in the light of my reflecting fame.

Glamorous it's not, lady. I thought to myself. But yes, it's the life I've chosen and it has its rewards. Yes, indeed.

The Perfect Moment, the Wrong Song

(Bucks County Courier Times)

NOVEMBER 4, 1987

Peter, Paul and Mary have spent a career celebrating America in non-traditional ways, but we never thought we would celebrate it in the most classic – singing the national anthem at a baseball game.

Not just anybody gets to sing the national anthem in front of tens of thousands of Americans. You have to have certain qualifications. You have to be well-known and lucky enough to be asked. People assume you know the words.

Robert Goulet sang it at a championship fight and clearly didn't know the words but he must be forgiven; after all, he's Canadian. Peter, Paul and Mary got to sing it at the fourth game of the World Series in St. Louis. When we were asked, we thought it might be a mixed blessing.

"The Star Spangled Banner" is not every singer's dream of a national anthem. First, it's hard to sing. It has a wide range of notes, an octave and a half, with one piercing high note. And although the first verse is passable poetry, you'd be embarrassed by the subsequent verses, which no one ever hears — and you'd want to forget them if you did.

The problems of singing this impossible song are magnified when a trio must sing it. Devising parts becomes a three-part-harmony nightmare.

One thing that happens in arranging a melody for three voices is that you begin to know and understand how the actual notes work.

In each Peter, Paul and Mary arrangement, within each harmony part there is a counter melody, created by the person who sings it. Each person must learn the melody in order to build on it, and that includes how the notes follow one another, descending lines to ascending lines and how the song builds to resolution.

Most people just remember a tune and don't think too much about it, but when you have to invent those harmony parts, you get to know the tune and its words very well.

Our national anthem is a war song, and in a way it's sad that the song that represents our nation should perpetuate the glory of war.

Perhaps that's why I always liked "America the Beautiful" better. It reminds me more of a Walt Whitman poem. It sings of America, the dream and its reality, not of a brief moment in our history which, God willing, we never will experience again.

But for the singer, what is more important is that "America the Beautiful" is singable. Now, singing in a ballpark is not a singer's dream of the perfect place to play. The reverberation of voice is such that whatever you just sang echoes back just as you begin to sing the next line.

Just imagine the old "Row, Row, Row Your Boat" with somebody out of tempo, and you'll get the idea. And to top it off, you're singing a song everybody knows. Now that's scary.

The thought that we just might make a mistake was too terrible to contemplate. It would be one of those moments that never could be lived down. The funny thing about musical arrangements is that you do them by sections, so that you really have no idea of the total effect until you're finished with the whole.

And then, although it may sound good in a rehearsal situation, the real test is in front of a live audience.

We had a chance to perform the song once before the game. And the strangest thing happened.

After 26½ years of performing, you get to know when a song moves people and usually why. We were in Des Moines, Iowa, near the end of a concert. We explained that we needed to have a premier performance before the one in St. Louis and asked the audience please to stand.

As the notes range out, the song's cultural magic began to take hold of audience and singers alike. The battle between sociologists and musicologist was firmly and irrationally settled.

What was it like to sing the anthem at the World Series? Absolutely, unequivocally terrific.

And it sounded pretty good, too.

CHAPTER 3

Motherhood, From Child to Grandmother

Alicia (left) and Erika pose with Mom after enjoying a country ride. (Travers Estate Photo)

BY ALICIA TRAVERS

When I'm asked about life with my mother, I feel it's a loaded question.

As I'm sure it is with most children's recollections, my childhood had both incredible joys and heart-wrenching moments. As a child of multiple divorces and having to find a nuclear family in the fallout, I have had my share of baggage.

Thankfully, I've unpacked it all.

I have no recollection of my childhood other than growing up as Mary's daughter.

She's my mommy. A woman blessed with great intellect and street smarts. Strong, stubborn, soft, and incredibly blunt. She raised Erika and me with a strong sense of self and an unbreakable foundation of ethics. She must have done a good job because we turned out very well, if I do say so, myself.

I can say this about my mom. I miss her terribly. Her soft skin, the way she smelled, and the sound of her gold bangles as she moved. The way she looked at me when I would come through the front door. It was the look of unconditional love that I had wanted to see and feel all my life but only truly felt the last five years of her life.

She wasn't without flaws, but she was always authentic.

I don't know when I realized she was famous. It seemed perfectly normal that people would politely interrupt dinner to express how much they loved her or what big fans they were.

My mother felt that the world of the music industry was not an appropriate environment for her children. There were no red-carpet events in my life, no picking up the phone to say, "Hey Mom, John Lennon's on the phone." Actually, if anyone called, it more likely would have been Senator John Kerry. Or that Daniel Ortega was at the door. Her musical fame didn't influence me at all. Her success as a person is a different story. I am most proud of her contribution to human and civil rights in this country and elsewhere. That's where she's a true star. The passion she had for social issues far exceeded her folk-singing fame. I admired her for speaking out and trying to make right what was clearly wrong.

I recall when I was about 19 or 20 and I was watching an HBO special called Skokie, starring George Dzundza. The long and the short of it was these neo-Nazis marched through the town of Skokie, Ill. The neighborhood is predominantly Jewish, and after the movie I was so angry this was permitted in the United States, I told mom that it should be illegal for a bunch of Nazis to march through a Jewish neighborhood and upset people. She agreed it was awful, but if we wanted to continue to have the right to march and protest for civil rights, we also have to support the rights of all people to protest. First Amendment rights don't belong to an exclusive club. She understood this fact because of her mother, Virginia Coigney.

Ahhh, Virginia!

■

"If Mother says no, ask Grandmother." That's what the sampler above her sink read. I have many fond and loving memories of Virginia. I think my favorite times were our sleepovers. It would be me, Virginia, and Better, the yellow lab. She would lay one of the outdoor patio cushions beside her bed, dress it up with fine linen, and Better and I would sleep right under her. In the morning, she would cook McCann's Irish Oatmeal the old-fashioned way, in a double boiler, *and* top it with heavy cream, brown sugar, and, of course, *butter*! "Everything is better with *butter*, dear." That's the family mantra. Another delight was Thanksgiving Eve. She and I would bake pumpkin pie together. To this day, I still make the pumpkin pies for Thanksgiving dinner and Irish Oatmeal for myself.

When Virginia passed, mom asked me what I wanted of hers. You see, our folks have a love for pewter. My answer was easy, I wanted

Better the yellow Lab's milk bone container – it was pewter. In honor of Better, a mini milk bone still lies at the bottom of the container. There is only one Virginia Coigney. My grandmother was a broad with a history and style who always spoke her mind. This chapter includes my mom's reflections on various stages of being a female, daughter, mother, and grandmother and relating to us on those three levels.

Mothers Share a Tradition of Protest
(Bucks County Courier Times)

MAY 10, 1987

Children can make you feel young and old in a minute of conversation.

One of mine did just that at the big march on Washington two weeks ago to protest American intervention in Latin America. Alicia, my 20-year-old daughter, was with me.

When she asked, "Who was that man you just hugged, Mommy?" I felt younger than springtime. It's being called "Mommy" that does it. My older and married daughter calls me "mother."

But when I told Alicia who the man was, she replied, "Who's Daniel Ellsberg?"

I felt positively ancient. Were the Pentagon Papers and Daniel Ellsberg's exposé of our government's lies about what it was doing in Vietnam and Cambodia so very long ago?

Looking at her questioning face, I realized it was a lifetime away; her lifetime, not mine, and it reaffirmed why oral history within a family is so important.

To share the same values, you have to share your experiences and your conclusions. Conclusions by themselves are not enough.

In 1983, I took my older daughter, Erika, on a human-rights commission trip to El Salvador. It was a hard and depressing trip.

A few of my friends thought I was crazy to take my daughter and expose her to a society as brutal and unstable as El Salvador's.

And, of course, they asked "why."

I answered: Because my country – her country – is deeply involved in supplying arms, advisers, aircraft, and American tax dollars to sustain a political and military structure in that country.

That makes it our responsibility as citizens to care about the effect of our help. But there was an even simpler reason: Whose responsibility is it to teach her to be a citizen? The educational system, in part, but mostly it's my duty. I am her mother.

You have to be informed to be an effective citizen. I took Erika to El Salvador so we could learn together, share something outside of our own lives, and maybe learn together to be better Americans.

I was arrested in front of the South African Embassy last year, along with my mother and Alicia for the same reason. Three generations in handcuffs.

During the civil rights marches in the '60s, I marched side by side with my mother. It was my mother who told me of the great labor demonstrations of the Thirties and encouraged me in the belief that peaceful protest was an honorable tradition.

We are not a family divided on the important issues of the day; we question them together. We share as intimate and precious moments those when we have stood up to be counted, together.

In America's complex and disjointed society, the lessons of our own history, both political and personal, are being lost.

The right and responsibility to dissent are deeply ingrained in American democracy, but like all traditions, it requires generational renewal.

My mother taught me to value accountability, responsibility, and continuity. So as I stood in the cold, wet Washington morning at yet another protest march, with my arm around my daughter, I told her about Daniel Ellsberg.

That's what Moms are for.

From Mom to Grandmom: Still Learning
(Bucks County Courier Times)

MAY 8, 1988

This may well be self-indulgent, but that's part of my current status as a grandma.

All grandparents I've ever met will talk about their grandchildren at any opportunity. Their pride knows no bounds. Say to someone, "You have a grandchild?" and you are buried in photographs.

Before I was honored with one of my own, I didn't understand the compulsion or the fuss. Ah! But now I, too, have joined the ranks of the besotted, bemused, and the grateful: grandparents. I, too, have photos. I, too, think mine is beautiful, sweet, and smart. I, too, am in love again. For that's what being a parent is about.

Children remind us that love is simpler than adults make it. That life is full of beauty and that some of it fills us with awe. That if one wants to have a good time, it doesn't take much. These are important truths, which sometimes require generational renewal. If you were too harried to learn these truths the first time around, you just might get a second chance.

Grandparents often are accused of spoiling their second-generation offspring. But even that, up to a point, is what should occur. A grandparent is a professional parent and by now should know what's really important.

Every child should have a grownup to turn to who loves him or her but is able to listen and advise without the distortion of parental vested interest. The child's behavior is not a reflection of the grandparent. It's important for a child to have an advocate in the adult world, one parents have to listen to.

Having said all that, being a grandparent is not an intellectual job. It's purely visceral. It feels good. They love you, you love them. Since you don't have them full time, their need for constant care doesn't wear you down until you're grumpy.

When you take a nap with them, they wake up happy to see you. They think you're special. You know they are. There is something so open and free about the love you give each other and so little worry attached to that love.

By now you've figured out that almost everybody has a little scar under the chin, eyebrow, or knee. That's life. But now you know that since your child has learned to survive, so will theirs.

By now you have a sense of your own mortality; your immortality is mirrored in your grandchild's smile. And somehow that softens the fact that you have a limited time here.

I've learned a lot since I became a grandma. Some are rather important things, like when to keep my mouth shut when my daughter does things a different way. She's become more understanding of me, when we do it the same. I love her in a new way, too, for now we belong to the same club. My mother and I do have a conspiratorial chuckle now and then when we hear my daughter describe the perils of motherhood. After all, we've been there.

We are four generations of women learning from each other. Perhaps the most important thing I've learned is just how lucky I am.

I think it's nice when people celebrate Mother's Day. We appreciate the thoughtfulness, but truly, it's been our pleasure.

Happy Mother's Day, indeed!

Growing Up a Woman in America
(unpublished)

Progress is defined in America by the social movements that sweep across each generation. But too often, women feel as if we are taking one step forward to two steps back.

When we see ads on television or in magazines for labor-saving devices, we know that they don't really "save labor" in the sense of giving women less to do, but instead just give women the ability to do more things.

Being a woman means being a worker on double shifts. We have always known this regardless of whether men choose to recognize this truth or not.

The economics of being a woman has always been demeaning and not by accident. But in these hard economic times, when single mothers and children are the majority of those living below the poverty line, demeaning has been replaced by shameful.

For women, this is unacceptable. Why do I say "for women"? Because we have the moral responsibility to change that frightening social forecast.

Last year, all across America, women entered political races for elected office. They were propelled to do so because successive administrations in Washington have proved for the past 12 years that women's issues are not of interest except insofar as it is possible to roll back the clock on women's rights. The appointment of Clarence Thomas was as insulting. Most women have had to deal with sexual harassment at some time or another.

If I sound a little strident, I come by it naturally.

I am the second generation of working, divorced, and, therefore, single parents. And whereas in my mother's day there was guilt and shame attached to those conditions, my generation knows you can be a splendid person, a valuable worker, and a great mom all at the same time. And I knew it before Murphy Brown. I also knew it wasn't going to be easy. Rewarding beyond my wildest dreams, yes, but not easy.

I married at 22, had a baby, and was divorced by 23. I got no child support and had no career. I couldn't even type. I was in serious trouble. I knew it and my mother knew it.

Fortunately, my mother had given me several gifts to last a lifetime. One was her love of books, the other was courage. Courage to risk. The belief that we women could be the authors of our own lives. The belief that we could overcome adversity, not untouched but intact. That's a gift I wish I knew how to teach other women, for once you've learned it, it's hard for someone to make a victim of you. She also gave me her belief system. Whether it's religion or ethics, children need to learn that every human being has a social responsibility to his or her community.

I took all this into rehearsals with Peter and Paul, two young musicians I had met in Greenwich Village. Ethics, folk music, and the baby. They had their hands full, I can tell you. And they were not yet what I would call "liberated men." Nice, a little old-fashioned for musicians, but all in all, pretty traditional. Meaning they didn't share power readily. A woman's place in music has always been articulated by a strangely muted voice. We have been the singers, the entertainers, but rarely the managers, lawyers, or recording executives. We have made the money but not managed it. Peter and Paul weren't ready to deal with me as an equal. I wasn't ready to give in. So we fought, we cried, we laughed, we grew, and at the same time we were becoming famous, we kept trying to learn how to become equals without killing each other. Needless to say, we all learned. We've been at it for 32 years.

The music helped us grow because it was about real things other than dating behavior. Folk music is about peace, the waste of war, and children's innocence. About love lost and love found. About dreams and nightmares. About the human condition. And always about making life better for everyone.

When the civil rights movement began, Peter, Paul and Mary was there, all three of us ready to lend our voices. Make friends with other women, network with them. Share what you have learned. We have gifts to give. In the giving, we become human in the best sense. And don't be afraid to sing. It does take courage but I've found it gives courage, too.

The songs we sang were already a part of the heritage of American democracy. I marched in Selma with Martin Luther King Jr. and my mother. Years later, I was arrested in Washington, D.C., protesting apartheid with my daughter and my mother. Three generations in handcuffs. I thought that was class.

That I became an activist was really not surprising. Between my mother's belief in the possibility of real equality in America and the positive nature of folk music, it all came quite naturally.

Through all this, I was learning about being a parent. Erika's first word was "taxi." She had been around the world twice before she was five. She was nurtured by day by Peter and Paul and Mommy and at night by a housekeeper who liked to travel. And in the end, I can tell you, unbiased as I am, she turned out great. Now she's a mother of two little girls of her own.

My younger daughter, Alicia, had a similar upbringing and is now a special education teacher. Wonderful daughters both. Somehow I learned to be an adequate parent, I guess.

It takes a lifetime to learn to be a grown-up. And just when you think you've got a handle on it, you have to start learning about loss. Loss of friends and parents. Loss of your own energy.

So what can I tell you that's of value? What have I learned that I want to pass on?

Learn to risk, learn to laugh, learn to get angry at injustice, and learn to fight.

We are special.

Hospital Visits
(*unpublished*)

The television set had to be unplugged and the videotape machine plugged in and attached to the TV. But the hospital set wouldn't unplug because they all ran off one cable. There was much shuffling around, and a young doctor was standing around saying, "What's going on around here? She's mad!" I was manic. I had gone this far, and the project had begun to take on a life of its own. It had taken me two days to locate a tape machine and then I had to pick it up and, by God, I was going to show this tape if I had to go out and buy a set. Fortunately, a lady down the hall had her own 21-inch television set, and we borrowed that. We plugged the machine in, popped the cassette in the machine, and I sat down next to my father and held his hand. Lights, camera, action – the tape rolled.

In the opening of the Mike Douglas Show, I sang, *The Song is Love*. Later, I sat down, and Mike said, "I hear your Dad's been ill." And I said, "Yes, I want to send him a get-well Valentine." I started to sing, and my eyes began to fill up a little. The cameraman had the instincts of a vulture; he came in so close that the picture was all eyes.

This was the first time I was seeing the tape, too, because I didn't have a machine to play it on, either. The tape finished. And the two of us just wept. We wept, and the doctor walked out of the room because he was weeping. We were all coming apart, and it was the healthiest thing that could have happened.

Then we began. We bypassed the past – the guilts and should-haves, the didn't-do's or did-do's. We went right in for what's happening now, and when we touched on the past, we did it without hostility or guilt. It seemed as though we just took that part out, because it didn't make any sense any longer. And after that I went to see him every week for about three months. Then I went on tour, and I came back and he was still hanging in there. He lasted much longer than the doctors had thought, 11 months.

Meanwhile, my mother had come to see him. They hadn't seen each other in 10 years. And they had a meeting that was like settling-old-debts time. She came with me one day. Earlier, she had said to me – she was very evasive about it – "Well, if it upsets you, I'll go with you." If it upset me? I had already managed to go several times.

Fortunately, I was smart enough to say, "Yes, it would be terrific to have you come." Then, in the middle of the week, she almost changed her mind. And then she said, "Well, I'll drive with you, but I won't go in." All the time, I was laughing and saying to myself how driven she was to go. She must have things to say. After 30 years, there are still things to say.

She hadn't seen the Mike Douglas Show or the tape of my excerpt. But everybody else in the world called her about it. She was driven, but she wouldn't 'fess up to it. So when we got to the hospital, I said, "Come on, Mom, let's go." "Well, all right," she said. And in we go. Well, I might just as well have not been there. They started talking about old times, old friends, a whole collection of memories.

At one point, my father said to her in that shorthand people use who know each other well and who have memories that they don't speak to you about, "I remember the hat you wore on our wedding day." Well, it was all-but-dissolve time. She remembered the hat, too. And it was like a metronome ticking back 36 or 37 years, dipping into the past. It was very Proustian, that hat, and for a fraction of a second it unlocked everything. It was just a line, but it had the effect of a fascinating book about people I didn't know. I saw their whole relationship as a young couple, he 19 or 20, she 18 years old. I had a vision of her as a slim, beautiful girl who didn't know she was beautiful. I saw her as a person, not as my mother. All that life and detail and texture from this hat with a feather in it. I still don't know what the hat looked like, but I see it as one of those 1930s hats with a short brim and the little feather. They talked about a lot of things, but what they were really talking about — and they said it — was: "Let's not think badly of that time, or of each other."

When we walked out, my mother was a basket case. She had gone through a catharsis of ironing out the wrinkles of a lifetime. It wasn't really a settling-of-old-debts time. It was more like answering the telephone. Because there wasn't a lot of time to answer the phone. It made her feel so much better.

And that was the beginning for me of a new relationship with my mother. She and I spent a lot of time together, and she became very involved in Dad's case. We could never get straight information about his condition. I'd ask the doctor, and depending on who his doctor was, you'd get whatever you got. Mother worked at the Danbury Hospital, so she would call Dad's doctor and find out what was going on. And then we would know. We were the only people in the whole family who knew what was happening. In a regular hospital, a terminal patient is a nuisance, so mother helped to get my father out of Norwalk Hospital and into Yale-New Haven, which has a special cancer research ward. The staff is all hand-picked, the hospital has fund money, and it's structured to handle the terminally ill. My father was on borrowed time already, so the change was for comfort and for any possible last chance. As a research hospital, they could try new drugs on him. That suited my father's purpose, since it meant trying something new. It was better than faith-healing, anyway. And it suited my mother's purpose, which was to see him in a hospital where she knew he was getting the best of care and the most pleasant people.

Over the entire 11 months, he'd been moving from the hospital to home and back again to the hospital. The last two stints in the hospital were at Yale-New Haven. He was sent home when he could go, but after a while, it became more than he or Beverly could bear. He had dwindled from a 200-pound, 6′3″ adult to where he weighed about 120 pounds. Beverly couldn't lift him out of bed. It takes two grown men to turn a body in that condition and not cause the person extreme pain. And there are bedsore problems. Eleven months is a long time to lie in bed.

So I was traveling up to Yale-New Haven on the weekends. I would spend the week in New York, then leave for my house in Connecticut on Fridays, and go to New Haven on Saturdays. Then at one point, I had to be away from the East Coast for about two weeks. When I came back, I called Beverly on a Wednesday to tell her that I was going to go

up to see him that weekend. And she said, "Fine, I'll see you Saturday."
Then she called back and said perhaps I'd better make it Friday. And
I figured he was coming down to the finish line. Then she called me
Thursday, in the evening. She said my father had gone into a coma and
I'd better come the next day.

I said OK and had myself a good cry. I got into bed, lay there
about 15 minutes, looked at Jerry and said, "He's going tonight. By 3
o'clock it will be all over." It was then about 11. We made it to Yale-
New Haven, from midtown New York, in an hour and 15 minutes.
Normally it takes two hours. We got there and had a hassle getting
into the hospital. It's not like waltzing into a regular hospital. It's a
research hospital; it closes at 9. But we did get in, and my father was
in a coma. Beverly was napping on a cot by his bed. It was dark with
only one small light on. He had on an oxygen mask, which made
horrendous noises.

We all sat up and talked – Beverly and Jerry and I. Beverly was
having a terrible case of the what-if's. What if we had done this, done
that ... And I said, "Look, Beverly, forget the what-ifs at this point.
You did what you could, and now you have to think about now and
tomorrow. The what-ifs are no longer relevant to your life. You can't
undo the past. It is what it is. Your best bet is to accept it."

I went on like that for an hour and a half. Then the nurse came
in. She was a terrific nurse, a bouncy, vivacious, cheerful lady, and
she knew how to treat the living as well as the dying. At 2:30 in the
morning, she was a blessing. She said to have a cup of coffee and she
checked his air. He was so frail, so translucent. All bones. He'd lost
his hair from the chemotherapy treatments. He didn't look like my
father, but he *was* my father. When you lose that much weight, you
become a mere kind of caricature of the person everybody knows or
chooses to remember.

Then the nurse said a wonderful thing. I don't even know if it's
true. It could have been the biggest lie, but it was the best thing

to say. She said, "Talk to him, he can hear you." She said that when people go into comas, they haven't the energy to be awake but they can hear you. If you talk loud and clearly into their ear, they'll register it. They may not give you an answer, or come out of the coma, or give you a sign of recognition, but they'll hear you. It was the best thing to say because you got to say goodbye. And I got up there and started talking, got a lump in my throat, cleared it, and said loudly and clearly that I loved him.

I had said my goodbyes, and we left. He died two or three hours later. I was right. He was not going to survive the night. You have an instinct that says move now or you'll regret having put it off. Death's not waiting for you.

The strange part of the story is that he had been writing a book. He was making bargains with God. First he had asked to live long enough to see his son into college. When he began to feel that was an unanswerable or unreasonable bargain, he asked to stay alive long enough to finish his book. And, in fact, he finished it two days before he died. He may have been holding on those extra, impossible months to finish the book. Some people can make those kinds of schedules for themselves. As he said when he went to New Orleans, if it doesn't work in two years, I'm giving it up. And he gave it up. I'll stay alive long enough to finish the book, and he did. It was another mystery book, but it hasn't been published. Getting a publisher is another question. He didn't ask for that.

I sometimes ask myself why, after so long a time, I felt such a need for holding onto my father. He was my father. He was my daddy. But he wasn't the daddy of my dreams. And, as a child, I was constantly trying to make fantasy connect with reality. Long past your need to have fantasy and reality connect, you keep scratching at it, out of habit. The telephone was ringing and I was unable to answer it. For some people, I suppose, the telephone would have stopped ringing after one or two meetings. There's documented research about what happens when people seek out their lost parents, and a lot of people do – more than one would think.

I remember seeing a series on television about adopted children who tried to find their real parents. Some of them realized after one meeting with their parents that they didn't have anything in common except some gene structure. Other people formed lasting relationships with their lost or abandoned parents. It's one of those up-for-grabs situations.

For me, the unanswered phone remained a missing piece of what I was. I wanted to know what my father was like, because I hoped it would solve a lot of mysteries about me. To put it on a slightly absurd level, I know that I always liked being Irish rather than English.

My father was Irish, and my mother was of British extraction. I never found anything romantic about the British, but being Irish was marvelous. If you were Irish, you could always say about yourself, "Oh, well, I'm the way I am because I'm Irish." You could blame anything on the romantic Irish in you. It sounds silly, but you are what you would like to think you are. Whatever Irish means in this sense is a fantasy, but if the fantasy plays a reality in your life, it is real.

Empty Nest
(*unpublished*)

1996

Alicia is leaving home and I hate it.

There, I've said it. I've been depressed for the last two weeks, as I face the most fundamental crisis in child-rearing since my kids' first day at school.

I have two daughters. The older, Erika, is 28, is married, and has her own little two girls. My younger, Alicia, is 21 and in her last year at college.

Erika left home at 24 to get married, and I suppose the trauma I felt was that she was old enough to get married. I sort of forgot that she would have to leave home to do that, and, besides, I still had one left.

They call it the "Empty Nest Syndrome," that depression that hits parents when their children fly the coop. These days, some modern-thinking people don't have children. They say they're not practical.

I agree. There's nothing practical about having children, except that having them forces the parent to grow up, too. When we were children, we believed the greatest myths about being a "grown-up." Topping that list was that grown-ups had external challenges, not internal fears.

Being a parent looked like an objective job. It isn't. It's a plunge into subjectivity, which on occasion is terrifying. When we are young, we are frightened about what will become of us. When you are older and a parent, you are still concerned about that but now you worry about them as well.

Children expand your sense of vulnerability, but they also expand you. You have to re-examine all of your values to define them, so as to explain them. You may even become a better person in the process.

It seems cruel that you spend a lifetime, prime-time, raising and nurturing children and just when they are capable of intelligent conversation, they leave home.

I liked those late-night confabs, sitting in our nighties on the bed. I liked solving someone else's problems rather than my own. I liked the intimate signals that parent and child share. I will certainly miss coming home and calling from the airport, telling her which airport, so she'll know how much time she has to clean the house.

I've loved being a mommy and I've discovered that I am afraid of not being one. It's been such a central piece of my identity for more than half of my life.

This is what it has all been building up to … nurturing a child to adulthood. This is the final step of hands-on parenting. From here on in, it's worry in private and give advice when asked.

So I'll help her move, try not to decorate her apartment or buy everything she'll need for it. I'll smile and adjust and remind myself how scary it is to begin, for both of us.

The Living Will
(unpublished)

1996

My mother is a young 70.

My great-uncle is 94 and going strong. His mother made 100, and if the genes hold true, Mom and I will have many years of quality time to spend together. But what if?

On a still-warm day, sitting in her garden, we found ourselves talking about old age, sickness, and death. And oddly enough, it wasn't a conversation that was depressing. Talking it out together was about as grown-up and loving as you can get, and it was uplifting and empowering. Because we were discussing the ethical approaches as parent and child with potential realities.

I hope my mother, at a very old age, will die peacefully in her sleep. So does she. She hopes that she will not outlast me. So do I. But what if?

More and more Americans are living longer. But in some cases medical technology can sustain life when life unassisted would surely end and should.

While they are healthy, some people are beginning to examine the legal ways to ensure the quality of their dying in case of some future terminal medical condition.

My mother said, quite adamantly, "I want no heroic measures. If I can't make it without machines, let me go."

We talked about what the organization, Concern for Dying, calls a living will. That's a document that can be given to your lawyer and your physician to ensure that you have some say about whether heroic

Travers Girls from the top)Mary, Virginia, Wyly and little Virginia. (Travers Estate Photo)

measures should be abandoned and allow you to die with dignity. We discussed what were a patient's rights. We talked about what she would want if she needed some kind of supervisory care and where.

My mother is an independent, dignified woman whom I respect and love. I owe her the preservation of her autonomy and dignity. She has written a living will and as painful as the possibility of her death might be, I will live up to her requests.

She'd do the same for me. And I'd expect the same from my daughters. Love is not just for the young and the living; the old and the dying need it just as much.

Mother Is Still Beautiful
(unpublished)

1996

Mother.

I brushed her hair; it gave her pleasure.

Standing behind her listening to her words careen about, not making sense. Requiring me only to reply as if all was normal. Words, her standard, now ragged and torn, the ironic symbol of her decline.

She who made a living with words, who defined her persona with erudition and wit, is now stripped of those essential tools.

The word-thief is dementia.

But she is still beautiful, still alive with feelings sparkling on and off like fireflies.

No sustained light now. Now I parent but not with hope. Her future looms, a darkening chaos. Holding in my memory snatches of hers, as hers are lost in the flood of dying brain cells. These moments are so hard. Soon I will be lost to you. But you were and will be safe with me.

My mother died in December of 1997. She had fallen into a coma and life slipped away. She had taken a much earlier train.

Who was she? I never really knew her.

I think I began to understand her when I was grown, but her truth was so well hidden that I sometimes think she herself no longer knew what was real. She was a good storyteller and like most, exaggerated a bit. She gave me so much and so little of herself that I take the scraps of her stories and try to lay them out, to patch them together, trying to make something that will resemble her.

My mother was born in St. Louis, Missouri, the daughter of Mary Jo Copeland and an unknown father. Why was she named — it always resembles a pattern with missing pieces of a cubist's vision — Virginia Allin?

Who was Allin?

Perhaps that was an old family name; perhaps it was the mystery father's. Without serious research, I'll probably never know. Mary Jo lived in St. Louis when she gave birth to my mother.

Life wasn't good.

When my mother was five years old, her mother committed suicide, leaving Virginia to be raised by mother's mother. Her grandmother did her duty, although it was made clear that she felt wronged by her daughter's actions.

A bastard was not what a good church-going Christian should be made to bear. Grandmother Copeland had had a hard life, losing two children because she was unable to nurse them, inverted nipples and pride. She didn't want a wet nurse, and it had caused their deaths.

Her two remaining children, Clyde and Mary Jo, had grown up with their mother in a little town in Arkansas called Piggott. My great-uncle described a small town with several churches, boardwalk sidewalks, and no fire department. Obviously between her grandmother and small-town life, something had to give.

My grandmother fell in love and disgraced herself and her family. Well, not all of it. Her brother Clyde loved her. And he loved the little girl she left. It was to him that the role of provider was to fall. I don't know when his father had died. But Clyde got a job as a salesman with a company up north and sent money home to his mother and her motherless grandchild.

What a dark beginning for my poor mother.

Sometimes I wonder if all family histories have chapters of Dickensian horrors. But I've learned that most lives are driven by a need to be connected. It makes it easier to connect if you know from whom you came.

CHAPTER 4

Foreign Affairs

Republic of Korea
(unpublished)

FEBRUARY 1985

The Republic of Korea, the formal name for South Korea, like all oppressive governments, would like to abuse its citizens in private. The American delegation that accompanied Kim Dae-jung back home sought to make that difficult, and it did.

As a member of that delegation, it was with shock and dismay that I read the newspaper accounts of the incident at the Seoul airport upon returning to the United States. Two of the major sources of information – the Korean government and the government of the United States – are guilty at the very least of misinforming the public, and that is a charitable assessment.

If only in the interest of truth, I wish to share an account of the incident from a third perspective, that of the members of our delegation.

Our group had been put together by the Center for Development Policy, a Washington-based foundation that studies the impact of American foreign policy on primarily Third World nations. Our mission was to accompany Kim Dae-jung back to Korea. Kim, a democratic political leader, had been in exile for close to three years, convicted of sedition in his homeland for being an opposition party leader.

When Kim Dae-jung decided to return to Korea, five days before the National Assembly elections were to take place, the government of Korea tried to dissuade him. They threatened him with imprisonment, then house arrest, and then perhaps not house arrest if he would delay his trip until after the elections. Our delegation volunteered to accompany him home.

The State Department and the Korean Foreign Embassy were fully aware of our trip. Further, they agreed that a small group of the delegation would be allowed to accompany Kim Dae-jung and his wife home from the airport. No one mentioned separate cars.

After we landed in Seoul, an official of the Korean government boarded the plane. He requested that Kim and his wife accompany him off the plane. Kim replied that he would prefer to pass through customs with the rest of the delegation as an ordinary citizen. The official nodded and left the plane.

After some delay, Mr. and Mrs. Kim Dae-jung, the delegation, and the press corps began to disembark. There were quite a few people in front of Kim and his wife, and several people surrounding him as a protective measure. This group consisted of Congressman Thomas M. Foglietta (D., Pa.); Congressman Edward Feighan (D., Ohio); Robert E. White, cochairman of the delegation and former U.S. ambassador to El Salvador and Paraguay; Patricia Derian, former assistant secretary of human rights and codirector of the delegation; and Pharis Harvey, director of the North American Coalition on Human Rights, among others.

The jetway was of the sort that turned sharply after a short, straight walkway. At the turn, there were curtains. Precisely as the first group off the plane passed the curtains, and as the second group off the plane which included Kim Dae-jung and his immediate companions disembarked, six or more men leapt from behind the curtains and surrounded Kim's group. They pushed, shoved, and punched those in front and behind Mr. and Mrs. Kim, successfully separating them from the rest of the delegation.

At no time did they identify themselves, even after repeated requests to do so in both English and Korean.

A group of about 50 unidentified men then rushed towards the group. Fearing an assassination attempt, those with Kim locked arms in a tight circle around him. Pharis Harvey was dragged and knocked to the floor; Patricia Derian was pushed, manhandled, and bruised; and Congressman Feighan was shoved to one side.

Still around Kim were Congressman Foglietta, Ambassador White, and two Korean-American citizens, one from San Francisco and one from New York. In the midst of the ruckus, a presumed official of the Korean government asked the Kims to enter an open elevator directly to the right of the jetway.

Kim refused to enter alone. A man then stepped out of the elevator, and, with a hand signal, sent the plainclothesmen into action. Four men grabbed Congressman Foglietta by the arms and legs and flung him to the floor. Five or six men grabbed Ambassador White, ripped him away from Kim Dae-jung and threw him to the floor. Kim, his wife, and two Americans were forced into the elevator.

The plainclothes guards then herded Ms. Derian, the congressman, and Ambassador White down an escalator. After a few minutes, a United States Embassy official appeared and helped them into a Korean government car, which took the four delegation heads to Kim Dae-jung's house. Contrary to the embassy's assurances, the delegation heads were not admitted to the house for several hours.

Meanwhile, the rest of the delegation, having been held in the plane and jetway until Mr. and Mrs. Kim had left the airport, was released and allowed to pass through customs. At no time was there an official from the government – United States or Korean – to calm our fears as to what was happening. All we knew was that the Kims had been taken violently, by whom we were not sure, and that the four heads of our delegation were missing.

We stood in the empty customs area with no one in sight and called loudly for help from either a Korean or U.S. official. After several minutes, an American Embassy official appeared. He explained that the Korean official at the airport had given him and his associates a bit of a runaround and had not let them pass through to meet us as planned. He did tell us that Mr. and Mrs. Kim were also on their way to Kim's house.

We then passed through customs and boarded a bus to the hotel to await further word. The question of assassination was clearly on all our minds. This obviously premeditated assault looked like what we had all talked about but what we had hoped never to see: violence, troops of some military nature, and no explanation.

Why was it necessary to use force? Why were we not allowed to speak to someone in charge? This was a planeload of diplomats and private citizens, not a foreign commando unit. Why, if the plans for our disembarkation were changed by the Korean government, were we not informed of it by the Embassy in Japan? Why not by the embassy when we were still on the plane? Why? Was the United States misled? Did the Korean government plan to handle it in this manner all along, or was there a deal that only the two governments knew?

I can only ask what was happening down those corridors of power that allowed Americans to be treated in that fashion, shocking behavior on the part of a foreign government towards the citizens of their strongest ally.

At the hotel that afternoon, we met with Ambassador Richard Walker and three other embassy officials. There was also a nurse present, on hand to give assistance to anyone who might have been injured.

Ambassador Walker was jovial and humorous. He expressed none of the serious concern that would have been the appropriate response of an embassy official whose countrymen and women had been assaulted and roughly treated. Needless to say, his unsympathetic treatment and quite obvious desire to gloss over the event insulted the delegation even more. He was patronizing, and ultimately engendered a similar response from us. It was a stormy and angry meeting

In the back of the room, Kim Dae-jung's doctor, Il Young Yu, attended an American Korean, Lee Won Kyong, who seemed to be injured. Later it was ascertained by Dr. Youn Song Kim, director of the trauma center at Holy Cross Hospital near Los Angeles, that the gentleman had suffered a mild stroke caused by the stress of the scuffle. Dr. Kim, an American citizen, went to the hospital and suggested that the man return to the United States to undergo tests. He left shortly thereafter. He pleaded with Ambassador Walker to recognize the brutality of the incident and the completely unwarranted behavior of the police.

At the meeting, the ambassador read a statement that was sent to the Korean Foreign Ministry and that was tepid at best, so couched in diplomatic courtesy that one would be hard-pressed to detect any note of protest or outrage.

A later communication to the Foreign Ministry seemed to grant more credence to the group's report. When the ambassador gave an hour-long interview to *The New York Times*, however, something had happened to change his tune. Now we were the "instigators of a media event."

The foreign minister called us "tofu heads" or something like that. This clearly was an attempt to discredit the delegation in the press or perhaps to shift the blame from the perpetrators to the victims.

One wonders why the ambassador did not seem unduly upset? Why wasn't he angry and insulted? Did he not believe us? Could his personal political judgment have colored his official judgment? Were his opinions purely that of an individual, or did he have orders, and, if so, what were they?

The leaders of our delegation called on the Foreign Minister Lee Won Kyong on February 9. The Minister denied absolutely that any of the events described had taken place. He expressed no regret. He did not inquire about the well-being of the member of our group in the hospital. He implied that we had not shown respect for the laws of Korea. Of the many things he did say, which were not true, was that Kim Dae-jung was not under house arrest.

In a later meeting that day with the deputy foreign minister, the delegates asked what the government had to fear from an anti-communist popular democratic leader. Sang replied that Kim had been convicted of sedition and invited the group to read the court's verdict. Since it has never been made public, the group jumped at the chance to see it, only to be told that the Foreign Ministry did not have the authority to release it.

The rest of the trip was pretty average for anyone who has visited repressive countries, which I have. We interviewed banned journalists, some of whom had been in prison, all of whom are on blacklists, unable to work. We spoke with church people who work with laboring communities, some of whom had been in prison. We met with the families of political prisoners, and observed the ever-present fellows in the back taking notes.

We went to visit the DMZ. For the record, the nicest Americans with the most realistic attitudes were the Army personnel assigned to take us on that tour. They knew their job and they did it well. The man in the back of the bus on that trip was from the embassy.

Many of us left Korea two days earlier than planned. For some it was *The New York Times* article of February 10 that made us leave. The headline read "Envoy Faults Americans." It is not easy to be in a country where the government is hostile to your presence.

I've done it twice before – in El Salvador and the Soviet Union. To examine human rights abuses is never a popular job. But when you also feel that your own embassy is clearly not on your side, prudence dictates that it might be a good idea to leave, especially when your group has already been attacked with impunity.

The fact that the government of South Korea believes that it can assault representatives of the American government and accompanying citizens is appalling. Many of us who were part of the delegation feel a little like the rape victim who is asked by the police what she was wearing and why she was there. For it is clear to us that from Ambassador Walker's initial response to our accusations against the airport police, to President Reagan's assumptions that mistakes were made on both sides, that the "line" has been to shift the guilt of what actually happened from the South Koreans to the delegation, lest our government have to censure an ally.

That may be "politics" but it is not fact. Nor is it just to protect the brutality of a military dictatorship by blaming one's own citizens. Nor is it good "politics" to send a signal to repressive governments the world over that it is open season on American citizens who may disagree with their policies. This delegation was not guilty of precipitating an attack. We were the victims of one.

At this moment, Kim Dae-jung is under house arrest, unable to see even a priest or a minister. The justification is that the government is protecting his safety, the same justification used to explain the necessity of separating him from members of our delegation. What danger did the delegates pose? What danger does his priest present?

What is truly dangerous for Kim and others like him is that there are people in the Korean government who perceive that democracy is a threat to its repressive government.

There they are right.

The results of the recent elections show that the people of Korea, despite threats of imprisonment and house arrest, are beginning to get the message. The government, therefore, will ultimately be answerable to the Korean people. As for our government, in light of President Chun Doo-hwan's proposed visit to the United States in April, a suggestion from the U.S. might be to see the full restoration of Kim Dae-jung's civil rights.

For me, that would be apology enough.

El Salvador
(unpublished)

November 1987

El Salvador has surfaced in the newspapers again … with her long-held answer to the need for political reform: Kill the Messenger.

Learning first-hand in El Salvador. (Travers Estate Photo)

Last week, Herbert Anaya Sanabria was assassinated. He was the head of the non-governmental human rights commission and the seventh holder of that office to be murdered.

I've been to El Salvador twice; both trips were part of investigations to study the effects of the Salvadorian military on civilian human rights and also to question the role that U.S. foreign and military aid plays in El Salvador.

In 1983, you could still see the body dumps. The Salvadorian government had, through various military agencies, murdered and disappeared 50,000 of its citizens.

The power structure of El Salvador still resembles something out of the 16th century – a rural country where 60% of the land is owned by 2% of the people. With this environment of feudal cruelty, there has been little chance for agrarian reform for the peasants of El Salvador.

The inquisition of El Salvador by the military and its death squads has destroyed the elements of society that might have called for reform and been able to accommodate it. Members of the university, medical profession, church unions, and middle class have been murdered, disappeared, or exiled.

The military was responsible for more than 100 killings a month in 1983; that figure dropped to roughly 30 by 1986.

The American Embassy deemed this a great improvement, enough of an improvement to continue American aid. It is hardly an acceptable number, for there can be no acceptable figure for political murder.

American foreign policy is part of the problem. American aid is a reward for anticommunism, no matter how brutal a regime; if it professes itself anticommunist, it is welcome to our economic support.

Since 1983, I have seen the improvements by the Salvadorian military in human rights become increasingly tied to public relations. Their military has been trained by our State Department to understand what, in a tragic sense, is the permissible level of human rights abuse. It would appear that the selective murder of 30 people a month is not objectionable because it doesn't inflame our conscience as a nation.

But make no mistake about it. The murder of Sanabria is a problem for the American conscience to consider. It is our tax dollars that pay the salaries of the Duarte government and train, clothe, and provide weapons for the military. Without U.S. aid, the government and the military could not survive.

So, sad as it is to say, we are coconspirators to these murders.

Guilt is not enough. We must declare to our allies and adversaries alike that political assassination is just not acceptable. We must declare it both in word and deed.

■

Mary Travers was in the Philippines as part of the celebration at the Aquino government's first-year anniversary. The essays below were part of a three-part series of exclusive reports she filed for the Bucks County Courier Times.

After years of Filipino strife, it's no easy walk to freedom

FEBRUARY 24, 1987

MANILA, Philippines – When I was 5, the "Japs" bombed Pearl Harbor.

The Philippines was a far-away place where "we" were at war. When I was 31 and touring Australia, I heard of how the United States had kept Australia free of Japanese occupation in World War II. But I never understood why the Philippines had been such a critical place then, or not until I looked at a map.

Their map, not ours.

The map of the United States, with xenophobic accuracy, places our country at the center of the world. And the map of the Philippines, true to its own nationalistic form, puts itself at the center.

Within 2,000 miles, one can reach Hong Kong, Hanoi, Beijing, Seoul, Tokyo, Singapore, Jakarta, and Australia.

Its military importance is clear. Its struggle for independence is not as obvious. Peter, Paul and Mary was invited to celebrate that struggle in a gala performance in honor of the Aquino government's first year. We were the only American artists to be asked. Our songs of freedom and justice had preceded us and were used in the protest rallies that marked the end of Marcos's brutal reign.

The desire for independence, freedom, and justice knows no national boundaries, and protest songs need no passport. So with briefing books in hand and a hope for Philippine democracy in mind, Peter, Paul and Mary began a very long journey.

The making of a democracy is not just implementing a constitution and reestablishing civilian control over the military. It isn't even the creation of an independent judiciary able to protect the individual from all those who would take away freedoms that a constitution guarantees. Those are the beginnings, the ideas on which any democracy must be built.

But in the beginning, as in the end, democracy survives and flourishes only as long as it addresses the basic inequities among its people. They must have the will, the leadership, and the means to make the idea a reality. For the Filipinos, there is uncertainty ahead, their friends are few, their enemies many.

Democracy hasn't had it easy here, and neither have the Filipinos. The last 20 years have been bitter.

Poverty, sustained and deepened by corruption in government and in the military, coupled with cronyism in commerce have all but stripped the nation bare. American foreign aid, both economic and military, has been systematically looted by Marcos and his associates.

The nation he led with U.S. help is left destitute. What remains to be done is a frighteningly enormous task, one that requires help from abroad and from within.

But within the Philippines all is not calm or of one mind.

Marcos supporters destabilize, community guerrillas still wage war, a minority Muslim population cries out for autonomy. Widespread hunger, disease, and homelessness are also common problems that this fragile new government will have to address.

My friend Ethan Robbins and I arrived two days before Peter and Paul.

No sooner were we out of the airport than the city and land displayed their uniqueness and condition. Manila doesn't look like any place I've ever been, yet it had parts of many I have visited. It is El Salvador, with its poverty, its shacks built of refuse.

The little jitneys that serve as public transportation are elongated jeeps that seat 12 to 15 people. They are incredible objects of folk art, each a little different, their polished aluminum sides unadorned by paint but decorated as if they were going to a Mexican fair.

We had been whisked off to stay at a resort while we waited for the rest of our party to arrive. Since all of the ministries we would be working with were frantically preparing for the big celebration on Wednesday, I suppose it was a combination of hospitality and convenience to let us entertain ourselves where we couldn't get into trouble or require a guide.

Whatever the reason, we left Manila for a day. We drove straight from the airport through the outskirts of town, through the flat farms, past rice paddies, up the mountainous and treacherous roads, and down again to the southern tip of Manila Bay, across from Corregidor Island and opposite Bataan.

In two hours, we saw the landless city poor, farmers with their yoked oxen, and, finally, the once-exclusive resorts of the very rich that now are open to the public. Our resort had not yet been open, so there we were with an entire facility at our command. This was not what I had anticipated.

I have traveled all over Europe, but I seldom think of recent wars. Rather, I visit the sites and ruins of conflicts long covered by earth and history.

But the first morning at breakfast I sat with my cup of tea, staring out at the island of Corregidor, with the high mountains of Bataan behind. Right in front, in the middle of the mouth of the bay, is Fort Drum, its rusted gun emplacements permanently pointed out to sea. The Japanese attacked from behind, by land, and the fort remains, a monument to a lack of military foresight.

I remember reading William Manchester's book on the Pacific war and being stunned to learn that more Americans died in the Pacific theater than in Europe.

Strange breakfast thoughts.

We fought that war to make the world free for democracies and paid for freedom with blood.

Forty-two years later I wonder if America will be as generous with her tax dollars as she was with the lives of those young men and women.

■

Contrasts reflect the Philippine revolution

FEBRUARY 26, 1987

MANILA, Philippines – We went up to Smokey Mountain.

I had heard of this place but had never seen it. It was not on the official government itinerary. So my companion, Ethan Robbins, and I asked an ABC-TV crew, Southeast Asian correspondent Mark Litke and cameraman Ron Dean, for a guided tour. Within a 10-minute drive of the Manila Hotel, one of the most opulent hotels in the world, stands Smokey Mountain, a giant garbage dump serving the capital city.

It was late in the day. The sun shown red through the smoke and haze of burning refuse as we made our way up the mountain of trash, which was set in layers like terraces. Perched on one of these terraces, we found a village populated by squatters who eke out a livelihood by sifting through the city's wastes, surviving on junk.

As we left our car, the rising stench enveloped us, instantly permeating our clothes and hair. Dirty children played in the paths, kicking a cracked, lopsided plastic ball.

There is, of course, no water supply. Every day, women set out on a journey down the mountain of garbage, carrying five-gallon jugs, to fetch clean drinking water.

Here on the mountain, disease is ever-present. Tuberculosis, dysentery, intestinal parasites – you name it, the citizens of Smokey Mountain have it.

The families sit outside their homes, chatting animatedly among themselves and watching the children. The mountain is not a safe place for little ones, I am told. In the mornings, when the dump trucks appear carrying refuse from Manila, the children rush out to be the first to find anything of value. Some of them have been crushed and maimed when the heavy flatbeds overturned.

Then there are the cave-ins.

As with the nation, stability on this "mountain" can be fleeting. In some places, the garbage is less firmly packed than in others. Children have been swallowed up when there was a sudden shift in the refuse pile.

Despite the misery, the people are not as I would have expected them to be, sullen and closed. Everyone says "hello" or "hi." I am not suggesting they are happy in their ignorance, but the Filipino people as a whole are gracious and unfailingly polite.

I chatted with a few of the families, just mother-to-mother stuff. A woman named Rose asked me why I had come to the Philippines. I told her I had been invited to celebrate the revolution in a big concert. She asked me if I was a singer. I told her I was the Mary of Peter, Paul and Mary.

There was a glimmer of recognition. She said, "Jet Plane!"

"Yes," I replied, and in the midst of Smokey Mountain's garbage village, the two of us sang *Leaving On A Jet Plane*. Rose knew all the words.

My experiences on Smokey Mountain stood in stark contrast to many other places I had visited.

This morning, Peter, Paul, and I went to the Presidential Palace, where we sang to President Corazon Aquino. The ceremony was part of an essay, poetry, and painting contest, held in the Philippines. An essay winner from the United States, Emily Joeson, 11, also was honored. After the ceremony, we toured the palace.

What a monument to excess and bad taste!

In the basement were cartons and cartons of cheap stuff: a hundred or so paisley Russian scarves, 50 white sweaters, all of them alike. Former first lady Imelda Marcos often bought up all of a particular item so she could be the only one with it. And, of course, there were the infamous shoes, racks and racks of them. The cost of just two pair equals what the average Filipino makes in a year.

In the palace rooms, darkness abounds: Wedgewood end tables with Louis XIV bases, a nine-foot romanticized magazine portrait of Imelda Marcos as Venus rising from the sea.

Another stop on the tour: a children's hospital, with open wards, where the young patients sit on rusting iron beds. As many as 34 children and their relatives may be jammed into a 20-by-30-foot space. The entire operation is overseen by overworked nurses, many of the doctors having departed for better-paying jobs in the United States.

Finally, we stopped at Malabon High School, where we were greeted by 3,000 students, a marching band, and color guard, all waving little yellow flags. This left us speechless. The school's generosity included a special lunch prepared for us by the teachers, an assortment of delicious local dishes.

So many images in mind as Peter, Paul and Mary prepare to sing tonight for the thousands of Filipinos at the concert and over television. We will join the Filipino people as they justifiably celebrate their year of victory, for democracy is hard-won and hard-kept.

But a very personal part of me celebrates Rose of Smokey Mountain, who can still sing sweetly and for whom the revolution has yet to be.

■

Huge celebration marks Aquino's first year

MARCH 1, 1987

MANILA, Philippines – The day began with the Mass.

Celebrated by Cardinal Jamie Sin, it commemorated the first anniversary of the revolution that toppled Ferdinand Marcos.

With pomp and ritual, Roman and revolutionary, this nation's mostly Catholic population prayed for peace, reconciliation, and forgiveness.

There were symbolic gifts offered. The cardinal had offered the body and blood of Christ to the people. They in turn, offered the symbols of their pain and triumph.

A member of the military mounted the steps and surrendered a rifle and side arm. The first political prisoner released from jail walked up the steep steps to the stage bearing a barbed-wire wreath of handcuffs, intertwined with flowers.

The 80-year-old publisher of the Manila Times, who risked his paper and his life under Marcos, climbed the steps giving an armful of newspapers.

The members of theater and television who manned the radio stations and broadcast a message "to take to the streets," gave a walkie-talkie and a tape recorder. Two of the many who had rescued the ballot boxes from tampering the day of the election delivered a ballot box, and on and on it went in revolutionary communion.

This was people power, a moment when the spiritual and the political breathes in harmony.

One couldn't help but say "Amen."

Then the president spoke to the throng.

Peter, Paul and Mary had been invited by the minister of tourism and the cultural minister. Peter had worked with her on benefits while she had been in exile with her husband, now the minister of agrarian reform.

There had been some disagreement among the organizers about Americans performing in what was a very personal and nationalistic affair.

And not so hidden in some of the complaints was some anti-American feeling. The United States supported Marcos right to the end. It is an unfortunate truth that to many Third World countries, the United States is no longer a beacon of freedom but more often a collaborator in their oppression.

The older people of the Philippines remember us fondly as liberators, but the young, who have grown up with the dictator Marcos are justifiably suspicious. This generation wants to develop a national pride and the last thing it wants is American colonialism.

But in the end the music won over nationalism, and it felt good.

We had gone to encourage and to share a dream: a dream that had propelled our hearts and bodies to march with Dr. King, to protest the war in Vietnam, to visit El Salvador and Nicaragua. The dream has taken me to South Korea with Kim Dae-jung, the Democratic leader so like Nemoy Aquino.

It had taken me to the Soviet Union to talk to oppressed Jews. For me, it is an American Dream and I'll joyously share it with anybody.

The performance was glorious.

The singers were all incredible. The Philippines is like Wales, a nation of good singers, actors, and performers. And protest songs galore.

It was a folk singer's heaven. But these singers were not just singing protest songs from the safety of a recording studio; they had taken their songs and their bodies to the streets. Not the safe streets of Washington, D.C., where the police have taken public-relations classes but the streets where the military uses its guns.

Backstage people were swapping tapes and addresses and telling those of us who had not been there that day last year what they had been doing, their hopes, their personal meeting with fear. I heard such laughter, joy, and excitement in the stories — stories that are still told with breathless wonder.

Hope is such a sweet state of being, when everything seems possible and maybe it is. That is the mood of the capital island of the Philippines.

As we left the campground, our camper was blocked by two packed cars on each side of the road.

A group of young men recognizing us began to sing *If I Had a Hammer*, with us leaning out the window and singing along as they lifted and very gently moved a car out of our way.

It was that kind of night.

Some estimated the crowd at a million people and some say two million, but they were all gracious, sober, and orderly, and that's just another one of the miracles in the Philippines.

At some point, I suppose I should try to sum it up: "Just what were your impressions of the Philippines and what do you think you learned, Miss Travers?"

I've figured out that the capital island of Luzon had a revolution but the bottom island of the chain, Mindanao, hasn't had one yet and the killing continues there.

Lord knows what's happening on the 7,105 other islands in between.

I know massive changes must take place or the communists and Marcos loyalists will keep agitating for violent change.

The new government has an almost insurmountable task of economic rehabilitation and the establishment of a pluralistic society, uniting a nation of separate languages, cultures, religions, and islands.

The Filipino people desire and deserve democracy and peace.

My fervent hope is that they can secure them.

Mary Travers was on the board of the International Center for Development Policy in Washington, D.C.

Nicaragua: 'A Lesson for the Learning'

(Bucks County Courier Times)

OCTOBER 31, 1986

A headline is like the tip of an iceberg, and if we're not careful, we just might collide with it.

But political issues are not like newspaper headlines that pop into prominence and then disappear, somehow resolved by their absence. These issues have a life of their own, whether or not we recognize them.

When Vietnam finally surfaced in the American consciousness, it already was a policy that had plagued two administrations, and America was trapped trying to rescue a corrupt government. In the end, we were corrupted by it.

Some of us vowed never to be taken by surprise again. We owe it to the 58,000 American dead and to their children, who now are eligible to serve their country, a vigilance born of experience.

In the early '80s, El Salvador was in the headlines. A brutal, uncontrollable military was running amok supported by U.S. military aid.

By 1983, the Salvadoran military complex was responsible for more than 50,000 civilian deaths. The country was in a shambles of death, disorder, and civil war. The headlines: "More aid for El Salvador."

When the United States props up a foreign government against the opposition of a large segment of its own people, we bear a direct responsibility to that country's people. And we bear a responsibility to our own.

We must not become the paymaster of murderers and torturers to serve our own global self-interests. Human rights is not a policy to be abandoned by pragmatic cynics in Washington who would deal with the devil in the name of national security.

The moment I read in the paper that we were sending advisers and military aid abroad, I heard a familiar tune. Three years ago that concern took me to El Salvador with a fact-finding group, including two U.S. congressmen and several former federal government officials, to study the impact of American foreign policy and to try to evaluate El Salvador's domestic policy in relation to human rights abuses.

I came home appalled and angry.

In El Salvador, I was not prepared for the grief of the mothers of the disappeared; not prepared for the squalor, hunger, and disease and the total lack of care in the displaced persons camps; not prepared for a country where the tiniest expression of dissent means death; and certainly not prepared for the complicity of the United States in these tragedies.

For as long as the U.S. foreign policy uses anticommunism as its only criterion for foreign economic and military aid and continues to deny the legitimate need for dialogue and change in those countries – turning a blind eye to government sanctions of murder – the more resistance movements in those same countries will reject the United States as a potential ally.

History is on the side of change – why can't we be on the same side? Why can't we demand a basic and traditional view of human rights as the collateral for our aid?

President Carter believed that, and many Latin Americans openly say they owe their lives to his adherence to that policy It is that basic belief in human rights that sent me in the last four years to the Soviet Union, meeting with *refusnik* Jews; to the Republic of South Korea, talking with banned political leaders, journalists, and union leaders; and to El Salvador again and Nicaragua this summer with Peter and Paul.

We arrived in Nicaragua, the second half of our trip, amid conflicting headlines: "World Court censures U.S.," "U.S. Congress votes $100 million to Contra aid." We met with a people trying politely to separate the individual North American from his or her government. We interviewed representatives of all the segments of the society (in a small country you can do that) from peasants to president. Believers and non-believers explained their vision of their country.

We met with the farming families of a little village attacked by the contras three weeks before; held the mother of a slain 8-year-old girl in our arms and cried; and visited the new graves of the 15 dead.

We were given an interview of extraordinary length with President Daniel Ortega – four hours over lunch at his home – where we were able to express our concerns about his government, ask questions about the closing of La Prensa and about human rights and religious freedom. He answered all questions put to him thoughtfully and, I think, earnestly. But in the end, what was important was not "how was he doing" but what our country was doing.

What became clear was that nothing the government of Nicaragua had done justifies the U.S. response.

The concept of what poses a threat to national security and what is a proper response is at issue here. These are two questions that need constant examination. The United States will be known by its deeds, not its intentions.

Is Nicaragua a real threat to U.S. security? I do not believe so. Quite frankly, Mexico, with its corrupt government, economic instability (which if it were to crash would bring the U.S. banking establishment down with it) and its enormous landless poor, poses much more of a threat. And Mexico is on our border. Are we planning to invade Mexico? What are this administration's criteria for arming rebels against established governments?

I distrust the selectivity of Ronald Reagan's foreign policy.

Two weeks after our return, Daniel Ortega came to speak to the United Nations. Peter and I, who live in New York, decided to invite President Ortega to an informal gathering and dinner at my home.

We invited 50 or so people in the media and members of the politically active community to give others the chance we had to meet and have their questions answered personally, by the president of Nicaragua. In attendance were the foreign ambassador and both the ambassadors to the United Nations and Washington from Nicaragua, President Ortega and his wife, the cultural minister. We talked and asked questions long into the evening. It was a rare and ironic moment in which the major representatives of a tiny nation tried to explain its hopes, dreams, and failures to 50 or so Americans.

A nation of 2.9 million people – 50 percent of its citizens 15 and under – trying to influence 50 Americans to stop the military and economic juggernaut of the most powerful nation in the world, poised to destroy it.

Needless to say, for days after, the press had a small field day on guessing who came to dinner. Chided or damned, depending on the editorial policy of the magazine or newspaper, I was who I ate with. Those are the old tricks of McCarthyism – guilt by association.

Reducing all political questions to us and them demeans and destroys legitimate questions and questioners.

That worries me.

I have no vested interest in preserving the Sandinista government; that is for the Nicaraguan people to decide. But I do have a vested interest in preserving my country's commitment to democracy and its political traditions.

To do that, you have to ask questions. I have and I didn't like all the answers.

Confusing Performance with Content
(Bucks County Courier Times)

JULY 17, 1987

For weeks, the American public has been subjected to a media blitz that addresses a particular political point of view, only one side of a complex issue.

The witnesses testifying before Congress in the Iran-Contra affair represent an extremely radical perspective. They have used the hearings to state their opinions repeatedly.

They believe they are justified in avoiding, circumventing and perhaps even breaking the law. They believe that despite the will of Congress, they know better because they are patriots. They tell us and show us with their words and actions that they do not feel accountable to the elected will of the American people, the Congress of the United States.

The world has been watching the earnest face of a man who believes simply that the military knows best. This is not a democratic notion.

Polls show the majority of those asked believe Oliver North was just following orders and that he told the truth.

What those Americans have not been asked, but must ask themselves, is the most crucial question that can be asked in a democracy.

Do you wish to have two governments, one elected but with no power to dictate foreign policy, and another, unelected, unanswerable to the people and able to conduct foreign policy as it sees fit?

If your answer is "yes," then you don't want a democracy.

Despite the well-prepared performance given by the witness wearing the uniform of the United States of America, he must be judged for what he did. The Nuremberg trials following World War II set a legal precedent: Following illegal orders is not a just defense. The Code of Military Justice also distinguishes between legal and illegal orders.

Regardless of our opinion of Nicaragua – and there are many opposing perspectives to the ones being aired – we must remember not to confuse performance with content. We must remember we are a nation of laws, eloquently set down in our Constitution, that define how our country is to be governed. It's been working very well for the past 200 years.

Whether or not we agree with the political philosophy of the witnesses at the Iran-Contra hearings, there is no place in our Constitution for the secret government of Lt. Col. Oliver North and company.

Soviet Jewry
(*unpublished*)

In 1983, I participated in two human rights commissions. The first was to El Salvador to study the causes and effects of human rights abuses in that country. The second was to the Soviet Union to visit with *refusenik* Jews to learn first-hand about the Soviet government's repression of Jewish religious and cultural life and denial of the right to emigration.

The two trips changed my life.

I had always been politically active, starting with the domestic civil rights issues in the 1960s. I had marched against the war in Vietnam, but I had never talked to the victims of human rights abuses outside of my own country.

And what people I met! People of extraordinary courage, many of them trying to illuminate their lives spiritually under terrible conditions. I remember Yuli Kosharovsky, 18 years a *refusenik*. A quiet Hebrew teacher who had suffered arrests and his family harassment, all for the right to embrace Judaism. I remember a priest in El Salvador who was in hiding from the death squads because he believed that peasants had rights.

These first two trips were very different, the abuses different, but they had "cause" in common. Both countries' governments believed that they could deny their citizens human rights in order to maintain the power structure of their country. They were both governments that believed that the end justifies the means, never having learned that the means become the end.

So at an age when most of us become entwined in our children's weddings, I became more involved, not less, in the world around me.

I spoke; I sang out against oppression; I got involved.

Since 1983, many things have changed, some haven't. The El Salvador that I visited again in 1986 was not different enough from the one I saw in 1983. Nor was it different enough in 1988. Today, El Salvador continues to answer the need for political change with military answers.

But the good news is that the situation in the Soviet Union is changing. In 1983, only 1,314 Jews were allowed to emigrate. In 1986, the number had dropped to 914. But in 1988, Soviet Jewish emigration had climbed to almost 19,000 — nowhere near the record high during the Carter détente years, when in 1979, 51,320 Soviet Jews were allowed to leave, but a real and positive indication that change can happen and is happening.

And there are other signs ... in Moscow, Leningrad, and other cities in the Soviet Union, there have been significant changes in the bureaucracy's attitudes toward the teaching of Jewish culture and the Hebrew language. Tourist exchanges, permitting Jews from the Soviet Union to visit Israel.

All of this was encouraging and was unimaginable 15 years ago. But it is important to note these have been policy changes, not changes that are defined rights by law. If for some reason the process of perestroika is perceived by those in power as not beneficial to the Soviet state, those freedoms now tentatively offered will undoubtedly be snatched back.

Change has ramifications expected and unexpected. The attempts to change a society from within the power structure, in the hope that change will revitalize a moribund economy, can be dangerous to those who initiate the changes.

What if the changes don't work? What if change threatens to destabilize both the government and the society itself?

This is what the leadership fears, in both our countries.

Most Americans believe that once a more democratic process begins in the Soviet Union, it will be universally greeted by its citizens as a good thing and in turn a progression of growth will continue.

But history has often said otherwise. Change is disturbing, and the reaction to it often creates dangerous backlashes. The quality and quantity of change will, in the end, be dictated by internal and external pressures. The quality of the pressure from the outside becomes not only important for those we wish to help, but for those Soviet officials who can make that help possible. Which means, my friends, having shaken the stick, we must also be prepared to offer the carrot; economic rewards to ensure that the liberalization process is perceived by its leadership and its citizens as a positive move.

The United States has used economics as the punishment; now it would make sense to make economics the reward. Make no mistake, a collapsed Soviet economy will protect neither Soviet Jews nor world peace.

What becomes clear is that as individuals and as a nation, we can no longer be satisfied with dismissing an entire people and their culture by hating and fearing their political system, as we have these long Cold War years.

No, we must do the more difficult, strive to understand them if we are to be of any real help. We have to be honest about what we want, what Russian Jews want, and what Israel wants. They may not be the same things.

American Jews have worked hard to convince the representatives of their own government to make the issue of the violation of the human rights of Soviet Jews an important part of any dialogue between Russia and the United States. To their credit, they have been successful.

But now we must embark on a much more difficult task. We cannot think that the fight is over. This is the most dangerous time because it is a time of "apparent" success. And many of us who have cared about this issue may feel that we can let up on this one and get on with others. Besides, it's gotten complicated and more serious. It's changed from an issue where we all could agree to give the Russians hell to one of responsibility.

We now owe responsibility to those who do get out; to aid in their resettlement wherever they choose to live, here or Israel. Responsibility to those who wish not to leave but remain loyal Russians – but ones who may, freely and without fear, also be Jews, as you are American Jews.

The premise that all citizens have the inalienable right to worship without fear from their government or their neighbors is the mark of any civilized country. The right to emigrate to another country if that is not possible, a fundamental human right recognized by the United Nations' Human Rights Charter. These issues are still at the heart of the question of Soviet Jewry, and they must remain in your heart also.

Tonight I am very pleased to address you, pleased because we can share the joy of victory together, for Yuli Kosharovsky and his family. Next week will be the end of a long and bitter battle.

For them the Passover dream will be realized, for them this year, it will be in Jerusalem.

CHAPTER 5

Up Close and Personal

My Abortion, Then and Now
(The New York Times)

AUGUST 10, 1989

In 1960, I had an illegal abortion.

It was badly done, and I almost died. I contracted peritonitis and survived only because of massive amounts of penicillin. The infection left me with a great deal of internal scarring and the fear that I might never have another child.

I was a young, divorced mother with a baby daughter. My ex-husband was a beginning writer with no money, so there was no child support.

Just as things really got desperate, I began working with two fellows who were trying to put a singing group together. I had always been one of those kids with lots of potential, but no marketable skills. Finally, the thing I actually liked to do, singing, looked like it just might work. I would be able to support myself and my young daughter.

But then I got pregnant.

To have an abortion was one of the pivotal decisions of my life.

119

Having an abortion didn't seem to be a choice; it seemed to be a responsibility to both the child I already had and to myself. Having a second child at that time would have changed my life and my daughter's. It would have thrown us back into what appeared to be a hopeless future. While Peter and Paul were willing to travel with one baby, none of us could have gone on the road with two.

A few years later, I remarried and, in 1966, I gave birth to my second daughter. I had almost given up hope that I would ever be able to get pregnant again.

Now I am the mother of two grown daughters and the grandmother of one beautiful little girl. Both my daughters grew up with the belief that they would be the ones to make choices about their lives and their bodies. A lot has changed since I was a girl. Furtive, often unlicensed "doctors" in dirty apartments had become a thing of the past. At least I thought so.

The Supreme Court's recent decision in the Webster case to allow state governments to pass a variety of laws restricting access to abortion is a large first step to overturning Roe v. Wade.

According to Planned Parenthood, there are approximately 1.6 million legal abortions annually in the United States. Twenty-six percent are obtained by teenagers, 33 percent by women 20 to 24, and 41 percent by women over 25.

Those numbers won't change if abortions are made illegal. What will change is the quality of the medical procedure for poor women, who will be unable to have abortions safely in public hospitals.

Some women will be forced to give birth to children they don't want and bring them into a society that doesn't want them either – a cruelty that doesn't seem to concern the anti-abortion lobby.

The "miracle of life" that those opposed to abortion rights wish to protect is clearly someone else's "miracle of responsibility." Although they give lip service to adoption, I don't see these groups giving homes to poor, minority children. If they did, I might feel their sense of morality to be a bit more genuine. Sadly, they seem unconcerned with the grinding poverty others must endure. Once again, the poor will bear the brunt of self-righteousness, enforced by law.

So what has the Supreme Court really accomplished in this decision?

It has created yet another division in our already divided society by affirming that there is one law for the rich and another for the poor.

It has also pitted religion against religion, the secular against the non-secular. It's a matter of religious faith, not scientific reason, that a human being exists at the moment of conception. Logic teaches us that beginnings are not the end result, they are only beginnings.

The court has also invited local governments to divide our nation into separate parts. Although it still remains a woman's right to have an abortion, it may become a selective right, depending on the state in which she resides.

The Supreme Court, on the day before July 4, 1989, our nation's 213th birthday, diminished every American woman's independence.

Score: Nature 1, Folksinger 0
(Bucks County Courier Times)

AUGUST 31, 1987

Another summer is almost over.

Once again I have fought the battle to tame nature and failed.

My flower garden is awash with the iridescent colors of Japanese beetles.

My lovely apple tree has a few apples that are almost ripe, but they are on the upper branches where the deer couldn't reach them. Neither can I. Nonetheless, I am hoping to find a way to beat the raccoons to the small harvest.

Connecticut country gardening is a treacherous and heartbreaking endeavor. If I were to compute the cost of home-grown food, it would easily match the budgets of most Third World countries.

I estimate that my tomatoes, for example, grown without those nasty sprays, cost about $100 a pound, which also was the size of the harvest – one pound.

My peppers succumbed to something that ate big holes in the leaves. The lettuce went to seed when I wasn't looking. My only success, as usual, was the zucchini; it grows despite my help.

The problem is figuring out what to do with a 10-pound zucchini. I know I was supposed to pick it when it was smaller, but it hid from me.

Like most gardeners, I also have discovered that deer aren't very dear to horticultural pursuits.

I have tried to protect my flower garden from the neighborhood herd by erecting a six-foot wire fence around my two acres of garden and lawn.

The deer did not take the hint. I found they can jump and crawl under it.

I wept aloud when they ate all the hosta and the lilies three days before they were going to bloom.

I've tried everything, including dried cow blood, which is supposed to make them think a terrible carnage had taken place. I also have tied dog hair and human hair in little bags around the property. Deer are supposed to be frightened off by either the scent or fear that they, too, could end up going bald. I'm not sure which.

Besides, it takes real courage to ask your barber or hairdresser for the clippings. They look at you funny, as if you're into voodoo.

I'm thinking of getting a life-sized statue of St. Francis of Assisi, so I can hide behind it with a shotgun.

But this morning several flower catalogs arrived.

The eternal optimist in me is stimulated. We all dream and order in hopes of the perfect garden. I am already forgetting about this fruitless season.

I am weak. I will read them.

If I had any courage, I'd throw them out and pave the lawn.

Book Speech
(unpublished)

1987

Some people learn to read only because school requires it. They never learn to love books, to need books, to devour books.

Long before there was television, lonely children found friends and escape in pages written just to them, or so it seemed. I was such a child, and fortunately for me there was a teacher who introduced me to the endless universe contained in books.

Bertram Benedict Standwick Mickelbank, how could I forget you?

Good teacher that you were, you tricked your students into doing what you wanted. You read aloud to us in the fifth grade. No one, young or old, can resist a good storyteller. That's tradition as old as humankind itself. Then you picked the perfect book, *John Carter of Mars*.

An introspective moment in 1968. (Travers Estate Photo)

As Edgar Rice Burroughs' serialized saga was spun, a roomful of 10-year-olds hung on every word.

And then you did it.

In an offhanded manner, you told us his books were out of print. Just as we began with horror to understand the implications, you added that we just might find some of his many works at a second-hand book store.

That day, many of us began a journey that has lasted a lifetime.

Our school was on East 11th Street, two blocks from Third Avenue with its rows of second-hand book stores.

New York is a poorer place without them, for they were personal places. Large, dark, cavernous stores, silent with the dry smell of dust, paper, and time, and in which there always seemed to be a sense of religious mystery.

Most were run by immigrant Jews, men who read and loved books in an earthy, direct way and who knew that to sell books you had to "know" your customer.

I can still hear their voices.

"Listen kid, I don't have any Burroughs right now, but I'll call around, and you come back in a couple of days. But hey, you like dogs?"

And so with an armful of Albert Payson Terhune, I became a book buyer. The trip from William James to Henry was swift. In high school, it was Upton Sinclair's *Lanny Budd*, which is better than James Bond. Then it was Jack London and Joseph Conrad, who pitted individual morality against nature and society.

The Russians, large and small, filled me with mettle and resolution. Thomas Mann's *Joseph and His Brothers* gave me the Old Testament with more than a coat of many colors; Edna St. Vincent Millay introduced me painlessly to poetry and pride; Bertolt Brecht and Richard Wright to outrage; and on and on it went.

I read, and they, those many diverse voices, spoke to me. The printed word is a patient adult voice and if I didn't always understand the full weight of what it tried to convey, it never rebuked me.

Sooner or later I would get the gist of it. I have reread some of those books years later and am amused and amazed at what I missed the first time round.

The value of books was articulated for me in a conversation in Ray Bradbury's *Fahrenheit 451*. The fireman asks an old man who collected books why books are important enough to risk his life for. He replies, "... That there is a tyranny to film, it goes at its own speed, and you must go with it. But a book can be read at your own pace, reread, and, most importantly, argued with."

Bradbury believed in the freedom of choice that books offer you. I, too, believe that.

My passion for books, which started as an escape from the tyranny of youth, ultimately became the tool that taught me that I could struggle against tyranny of any kind.

God bless you, Mr. Gutenberg.

Graduation Blues: What Comes Next?
(Bucks County Courier Times)

JUNE 9, 1988

I'm thinking of writing a new folk song called "Graduation Blues."

It has all the essential elements of good drama – pride and fear, loss and success, nostalgia and hope – and all at the same time.

They say that being a parent is a mixed blessing. It isn't. A mixed blessing would imply more than one blessing. In reality, being a parent is a mix – a blessing and a curse.

The blessing part is indescribably sweet and personal. It gives life a profound meaning.

The curse aspect is very describable. On occasion, children are selfish and insensitive to anyone's need but their own. Despite that, you still love them.

Being a parent makes one particularly vulnerable to slights of offspring. Armed with this inborn knowledge, children can be your most effective torturer.

They are most dangerous when they perceive themselves to be cornered. It's then they bite the hand that feeds them. I am told that the last 10 years of parenting are the hardest and I'm convinced it's true. Gone are the days when I couldn't get them to eat salad but I could get them to do everything else. Gone are the days when I had all the answers to their questions or understood their fears and when I had enough control to keep them safe.

Now I have sleepless nights worrying about what they are worrying about. Now I have some answers but I am afraid they won't believe me and want to find out for themselves. Suddenly I realize that "parenting" young adults is going to be a very different business.

My youngest child is about to become an official adult. And it scares us.

Alicia is graduating from college. Classes already have ended and all that's left is the ceremony. We are proud and excited, shopping for the dress, planning the party.

But the other night, Alicia and I had a curious argument. I said something I thought was innocuous; she overreacted and we both felt hurt. It took me a few hours to figure out what the fuss really was about. She's frightened.

Gone is the job she's been working at for 16 years. In its place is uncertainty. I know that this is only the beginning of new challenges and that part of being an adult is knowing you can survive uncertainty.

I know there are times when you just have to leap off the cliff and life will produce opportunities and choices.

I know that skills you hadn't thought you had will appear and be developed. But those are the kinds of things she'll have to learn by herself.

And knowing those things doesn't stop them from being scary.

It's at times like these that the pain of parenting is acute, and I begin to appreciate the wisdom of age.

I know from experience that I am stronger and more resourceful than I ever imagined I'd be ... and so is she.

When you understand the past, you can predict the future.

A Very Grown-Up Day
(unpublished)

1995

"Ah, Mom, please. We'll take care of her, walk her, feed her. Please, Mom?" my two daughters said of the wiggling mass of black puppy at their feet.

I don't know why I said yes. Fatigue or perhaps a moment remembered of my own childhood and a dog I had loved. But that's the way it was.

Now, there we were again on the same lawn in the country. The girls all serious and grown. One a mother herself and the other a schoolteacher. They sat with the same sweet dog, now 16, gray-muzzled, and silver-eyed.

It was her last day.

We had come together to say goodbye and ease her out of a world she had made richer by her presence. We would be together as a family, for she was our family's dog. The hole was dug and we were waiting for the vet who had agreed to come to us. We wanted to avoid the panic Sasha always felt at the vet's. She had been there too many times in the last few weeks.

There comes a time when the decent and kind thing to do is to put an end to an animal's suffering. That's what everybody says. But when it's your pet, it's hard.

Sasha had been a very special animal.

Three years after we got her, my older daughter left home and moved to Greenwich, Conn. My younger graduated high school and then college. Got her master's and will be moving to Connecticut this fall. Although the girls had their own lives, Sasha, loved by all, was still cared for by all. When my husband and I traveled, Sasha would stay with one or the other, a constant in our collective lives.

And now we were to be together on her last day.

As we sat on the patio eating a late lunch, Alicia pointed out that no one would have an appetite later. She was right. Sasha, who worked the table as the professional she was, begged for whatever it was we were having. Not potato salad, I thought. But Erika heard my unspoken comment and said, "Why not?" as she gave the dog a piece. It was a moment of black humor, but, of course, why not?

The worst moment was when our vet arrived. Sasha, who seldom barked, began to howl. It was as if she knew. Tears from three pairs of blue eyes trying to be stoic. My husband turned away. But the pain was evident. For she had become his dog.

The vet, a young woman from North Carolina with a sweet, Southern way of speaking, said calming things, and gave Sasha a shot of some heavy sedation. The family went up on the lawn to have some private time with our dog as she began to relax. And then unable to stand, lay down.

Erika took a pillow off one of the lawn chairs and put it under Sasha's head. The four of us, my husband and my two daughters sat surrounding our old friend, petting and crooning comforting words. Soon she was barely conscious. She was ready and we were swept along by the process and our pain was as ready as it could be.

Dr. Stanland and her assistant came up and sat down with us. Nothing rushed, but slow and dignified. She explained what was to happen next. A needle in the leg and she slipped away. We all sat there for a while, petting her face and ears. So silky, we used to call them her veal scaloppini ears. We were all crying silently. Erika got up and lined the hole with a pretty sheet. My husband looked up at me and said solemnly, "A grown-up day."

Ethan gathered Sasha like a child into his arms and laid her gently into her grave. Erika covered her with the sheet and Alicia took the first handful of dirt. We all laid a hand full of dirt and cut roses from the garden and thanked her. We all took turns filling the hole and laying rocks on top. The sun was slipping over the hill. A moment of glorious gold afternoon light and then dusk.

Sasha had been a part of my children's last years as children. Once we had all lived together as a family. Now they were grown and had independent lives, and Sasha somehow was a symbol of that childhood. We had all been young together, and now we had entered another level of family. We had been loving and responsible together.

A very grown-up day.

When More Than Decorations Are Stale
(Bucks County Courier Times)

JUNE 28, 1988

There should be some kind of law against displaying holiday decorations out of season.

It was just after Thanksgiving when my neighbors put up a large blow-up Santa, complete with reindeer and sled. It lit up at night making it look as if it was celebrating the opening of a fast-food store instead of the holiday of giving.

When you live in a small town and drive down the same country roads, you get very proprietary about the land, the trees, and the houses. You feel parental when someone decides to fix up his house. Glad someone cares.

Now I understand that taste is a very personal thing. People know what they like and often it's very different from person to person.

I noticed at Christmas that around my neighborhood people get very creative about the outside.

Fresh green wreaths on doors, delicate lights strung or wrapped around the branches of trees. While gaily wrapped gifts are being hidden from curious children, the festive spirit is shared openly with the community. Some of the decorative decisions weren't my taste, like the giant plastic balloon of Santa, but they have small children who must have gotten a kick out of it.

I thought it was hideous and junky. But it's only for a little time, I thought. Christmas came and went, but it stayed. Easter arrived and though it had lost a little air, it was still there. I thought when they put the plastic Easter eggs near their mailbox that Santa surely would be put away. But by the end of April, with daffodils standing bright and wisps of forsythia waving in the spring air, Santa was still slumping on their front lawn.

Now I don't really know these people except to say hello. So the idea of asking them to take the thing down seems intrusive. The longest talk I've ever had with them was about our cars. We both had the same kind and both had trouble with them. But they'd just bought a new one and so I thought maybe I'll just ask them if they like it, then subtly ask when they are going to sack Santa.

So I did.

Feeling sheepish (I always do when I am saying one thing and meaning another), I dropped into the conversation, "Gee, it's spring ... the flowers look so inviting after the long winter. Santa's a little out of style now, isn't he?"

They looked surprised. They said they hadn't thought much about it, but supposed he did. The Daddy looked down at his kids and asked if it was OK to take Santa down. The children didn't look thrilled but they hadn't thought about it either. I got the feeling Santa might be a permanent shrine and I was outnumbered.

But the next morning, as I worked in the flower bed, I noticed Santa at last was gone.

I was glad but somewhat uncomfortable at the same time. I felt I had intruded into my neighbors' space, but I also felt they had intruded on mine.

Being right is not always satisfying.

Some sort of agreement about holiday decorations would make things a lot easier. They should be just for the holiday period, not to be left out indefinitely. People decorate to share a sense of festiveness, but stale decorations – left out past their time – become visual litter.

Christmas decorations in December are an act of sharing. In the spring they are a sign of bad manners.

A Fight for Recognition
(Bucks County Courier Times)

NOVEMBER 11, 1987

World War II is over, but a battle still rages to determine who its veterans were.

The Marine Engineers Beneficial Association, an affiliate of the AFL-CIO, brought just such a lawsuit against the Pentagon last year.

Last month, federal Judge Louis Oberdorfer in Washington, D.C., ordered the Department of Defense to reconsider its earlier decision to deny veteran status to men who sailed as merchant seamen during World War II.

Hollywood has glorified the stories of the various armed services involved in America's wars, but the invaluable service of the Merchant Marine is one that has yet to be acknowledged.

They were the civilian seamen, under the control of the Navy, who transported everything from planes and tanks to the food that sustained both our civilian and military allies.

Their war began before Pearl Harbor, and by the time the United States had formally entered war, six American merchant ships already had been lost.

Judge Oberdorfer's opinion cited the grim fact that the percentage of deaths for merchant seamen in the first year of the war was higher than that of any military service.

One of the reasons for the high death rate was that merchant ships, in the beginning of the war, were both unarmed and unescorted.

During the war years, an estimated 250,000 men served in the Merchant Marine. Seven thousand died. Some died on burning ships, some in the water, and even a few in Japanese prison camps. There are no records kept by the government on service-connected injuries or disabilities.

If veteran status was awarded, the men who served and who still are alive would be eligible for selected veterans' benefits, such as home loans and burial in a national cemetery. But the most important reason for giving merchant seamen veteran status is simply that the government would be awarding those men an honor they already have earned.

The American Legion and the Veterans of Foreign Wars oppose giving the merchant seamen veteran status, the very men who owe their lives in part to those civilian seamen who risked theirs to support them. There is a tradition of service rivalry, but veteran status should not require a club tie.

My father, Robert John Travers, joined the Merchant Marine in 1939 and sailed as a first mate, off and on until 1953. He was a writer as well, first as a journalist. That's how he and my mother met, when they both worked for the same paper.

During his years at sea, he wrote several novels, one about seamen and the union and one about the war in the North Atlantic on a merchant ship.

He sailed in convoys to Murmansk, Russia, twice during the war. It was a treacherous run. The merchant ships had to skirt around

Norway, Denmark, and Sweden, all held by the Germans. If you hit the water in that part of the North Atlantic, you froze in less than three minutes. When people speak of the Murmansk run, they recall its enormous cost, 80 percent losses. He lived to tell about how it felt to be a statistical longshot.

Years later, when I was still in high school, my father took me to see his ships. We stood on the Jersey side of the Hudson River, looking down at the rows of old Liberty ships at anchor. Side by side there must have been hundreds of them appearing ghostly, without their crews. A few were being used for grain storage.

He recalled their construction, the furious rush to produce them, how they were welded instead of riveted, which caused some of them to literally fall apart at sea.

You could tell he was fond of those old ships. Then, in his quiet voice, he told me that he'd rather see them unused, for as long as those ships were not in commission we were not at war.

My father died of cancer in a New Haven hospital in 1974. It was a long, hard death with plenty of time to review his life and what he had done with it.

He never doubted he had served his country, and neither do I.

CHAPTER 6

The American Left

(unpublished)

For young people who are not particularly active in liberal politics, it's important to explain where the American left came from. The people who were attacked in the 1950s by Joe McCarthy had been young people in the 1930s. The Thirties were years when the American system, for all its ideals, was not working.

The Depression didn't mean that the ideals of the system were wrong, but one critical thing can throw a whole system out of whack. No matter how high your ideals are, no matter how far-reaching the idea of your nation is, it doesn't stand a chance of succeeding if you don't take care of certain problems. Those problems can break a nation's back, because morality on paper is not enough.

The people who came out of the Thirties, out of the Depression, had witnessed a system in disarray. Yet they were forged with an idealism that was to America's credit. After all, we didn't seek to solve the economic problem of the Depression by external expansion. We agreed to solve the problem by working internally.

The government made an effort to create jobs. The government tried to serve the people in a time of economic ruin, just as in a time of national defense the people must serve the government. The idealistic people who grew up in the Thirties knew that things were wrong and had to change. But you cannot train people to wrench change out of chaos and then defuse them when you think everyone's had enough change. People don't work that way. Change is a very exciting, heady business, and it's what life is about. The attempt to defuse the idealists led to disillusion. They were first disillusioned by the way Europe was carved into spheres of influence after World War II. Then the political groups that had been forged in the Thirties began to consolidate their power and feel comfortable, and they fell into the trap of what power does to people. The unions lost their vitality because of the fears that grew out of the Cold War and McCarthyism. Overnight, unions kicked out anybody with left-wing tendencies.

Communism was considered the same in every place. That was a ridiculous error made by people who didn't study history. No two democracies in the whole world had ever resembled each other. Why should communist governments be different? A system of government takes on the flavor of the culture and history of its country.

Chinese communism is nothing like Russian communism. Cuban communism is totally different from the first two. The French communists don't speak to the Russian communists half the time, and they certainly don't speak to the Italian communists. In an international sense, one can be a communist and not agree with any of the other communists. But John Foster Dulles didn't believe that. He believed that all communism was the same and it was going to gobble up the world.

American communism had a very American flavor. The American communist of the Thirties and Forties was still filled with the feeling that, potentially, America had it made. The main problem was making life fairer for everyone. American communists were never as realistic as European communists. But then I suspect that American politics were never as realistic as European politics. We haven't been here that long.

CHAPTER 7

Stage Talk: Mary's Monologues

Passing the Comedic Torch

By Noel Paul Stookey

When Peter, Mary, and I became the Peter, Paul and Mary trio in the early '60s, it was pretty much understood among the three of us that we were contributing individual gifts to a collective voice.

Peter's clear and pure tenor, Mary's dynamic contralto and my wide-ranging baritone encouraged us to create highly personalized harmonic voicings considered by some as unorthodox but by us as perfect for a particular lyric or song.

Beyond these mutual musical decisions, there were performance responsibilities that also seemed to fall most naturally to one or the other of us. At the start of our career, our limited song repertoire barely numbered a dozen. Many of the first engagements were structured so that the trio would open with three or four songs followed by the three of us doing solos and then a final group of trio songs to conclude. That format ultimately became the pattern for 50 years of performance: first half trio, second half beginning with the three solos, and the group reassembled once again at the close.

For my solo, it was always easy, this being funny stuff. In my Michigan high school, I was often chosen to be the master of ceremonies, and, while preparations were being made behind the scenes, I would stand out front finding ways to fill way too much time with way too little information. On stage, my version of the Mickey Mouse club song became a '50s rock 'n' roll ballad and, following my imitation of a young child invited to entertain at his mother's bridge party, I would recreate the sound of a toilet flushing as an old American standard.

The '50s and '60s were a time of great comedic transition. The era of classic "joke tellers," like Bob Hope and Red Skelton, was displaced by the outrageous antics of Jonathan Winters, the dark perceptions of Lenny Bruce, the intellectual subtlety of Mort Sahl, the awkward introspection of Woody Allen, and the provocative paranoia of Shelly Berman. Most of all, it was a deliciously exhilarating unraveling of hypocrisy and presumption – no matter where it was found – in politics or attitudes.

Because of our solo performing experience prior to the formation of the group, Peter and I were most comfortable doing a majority of the introductions. (Mary would later confess to audiences that our manager Albert Grossman had suggested that she *not* speak so that she could maintain an on-stage mystique.)

"…and I *believed* him!" she would say with hands on hips in mock exasperation.

While my one-liners and Midwestern affability might often be appropriate for relaxing an audience or defusing a tense on-stage microphone failure, Peter became the "go-to" guy for the serious introduction. His earnest focus expressed best our collective thought – whether explaining a political position or introducing a sensitive ballad.

Still, over a five-decade span of performance, a subtle and gracious rearrangement of our onstage roles occurred.

Noel and Mary putting their comedic heads together.
(Photo by Robert Corwin/robertcorwin.com)

Perhaps it was in part because of my spiritual reawakening in the late '70s that I began to speak out on more serious issues when PPM reunited in the late '70s. By that time, Peter had become a father of two and was developing a talent for engaging in play with his children on a level that easily translated to a more laid-back — sometimes goofy — stage presence. And thanks in part to her six years as a solo performer during our "time off" from 1971 to 1977, Mary had reclaimed her speaking voice.

She began to take risks on stage and trust her instincts. Her introductions to songs like *Blowin' in the Wind* and *Where Have All the Flowers Gone?* revealed both an intelligent and insightful femininity. Following the birth of her grandchildren, she seized upon the occasion (as she maintained *any* grandmother would) to present the concert audience with a "photo of her grandchild" enlarged to such a size that that everyone in the hall — even in the balcony — could see and share in her pride and enthusiasm.

Although Mary's solo section always concluded gracefully with a song or two, her natural bent for social commentary began the moment she approached the microphone. Her impatience with modern gadgets caused her to speak out about cellphones, computers, calculators, video recorders, and especially anything designed with buttons smaller than her fingers or labeled in print so microscopic that she threatened to hire a teenager as a personal high-tech translator.

Though audiences greatly enjoyed her on-stage Luddite persona, she nonetheless recognized the importance and the opportunity the new technology offered and, in 1990, after a couple of stumbling self-deprecating weeks, she had mastered the use of one of the first portable computers. Her articles, from around the globe and transmitted agonizingly slowly through phone lines via a 300-baud modem, began appearing as columns under her byline in the *Bucks County Courier Times*, an award-winning Philadelphia suburban daily newspaper that became her journalistic home.

Finally it seemed to me she was accepting the full range of her gifts – not only speaking with ease to thousands from a concert platform, but beginning to reach hundreds of thousands through her inspired and inspiring writings.

Following are some of Mary's on-stage solo monologues.

■

St. Louis
The Addition

SEPTEMBER 22, 1991

We so rarely are in a city for three days. Life has come to mean touring one-night stands. So we really sort of get to do the things we most like to do. . . I, of course, have a black belt in shopping.

I thought the placement of our hotel at the Hyatt at the old train station was great. And for me, to be able to fall out of bed with my credit card in my hand, was really something. I really liked that.

When your arms were full, you didn't have far to go to get rid of it. That was great. But that's a very dangerous mall. I managed to do a little damage. I'm not quite sure how I am going to get home with all of it, but I'll manage. I'll let Noel carry it.

For years, he used to have to carry the hanging bag. We used to call it the death bag. You know what a man's suit bag looks like.

Well, women's bags are really a little longer. And if you have long stuff you don't want to get wrinkled, they are very long. Which means that now Noel won't carry it anymore because he says it's bad for his fingers.

We have a road assistant who carries it. One of the requirements in the interview is height. Because if you are like this, short, you drag it.

I knew you would be fascinated with that piece of information. Just a little inside look at traveling.

We are going home tomorrow. This is the end of the summer tour. And we have three weeks off. So if we are excessive, strange, and funny, it's because we're excessive, strange, and funny.

I have had a very exciting year this year doing something I've never done before which was to call up a builder and make my house bigger. We added a room on to my house.

The moment I started to discuss it, all of my friends said, "Oh, let me tell you about the things we did. And how much it cost. More than it was supposed to cost."

I said, "Now, listen. Don't tell me horror stories. This is not going to happen to me. I've known this builder for 26 years. We went over the figures very carefully. We even built in a little fudge area in case in the building of the foundation we struck oil. Or conversely had to blast."

He promised that it wasn't going to cost anything more than what he said it was going to cost. And I believed him. And he lied. And it went way over.

I won't say that I'm grumpy. Insanely angry, I guess. Grumpy, no. I'll kill him.

But what really made me mad is I had just sorted out how much this new room was going to cost. And how much it was going to cost to repair the kitchen, which they had destroyed getting to this new room.

They had torn up the floor to run the heating ducts through. They had torn up a wall to run electricity.

I mean they made a bloody mess. And now, I didn't have the money to repair the kitchen and I went to my accountant and asked for the money. And he said "no."

I said, "I have to fix the kitchen." You see, I was also planning to do something else. I was planning to get married. And I wanted to have the reception at the house. Now, his relatives have never seen me. Never seen the house, the kitchen. They are going to think I live that way.

I have to fix the kitchen. The accountant said, "Later." Now, he doesn't realize to whom he is speaking. I am the queen of instant gratification. Don't give me "later." Later is not in my vocabulary. So I did what any red-blooded American woman would do. I called my girlfriends.

One of them knows what she's doing. And she arrived with tools and a truck, little levels with bubbles in them. And my favorite, a table saw. Oh, I want one for Christmas. This truly is a great instrument. But I want lessons. I mean, I don't play the guitar, so if something happens, it's not a disaster. But, they could nip you.

Anyway, there were five of us. So there were five of us who had absolutely no idea what we were doing. But we were willing to follow Kathleen. We got her a tee shirt that said, "She who must be obeyed."

And we began.

We started with the ceiling. I decided I didn't like the ceiling. It was too low. And, why not follow the roofline? Why not? So we tore the ceiling out in 20 minutes.

It was great. I missed my calling. I should have been in destruction. Oh, this is better than therapy. Tear it right out.

Then there were these little pieces of wood that went across the ridge line of the roof that the ceiling used to hang on. And we took those out, too. Every time I say that, some man comes backstage, and says, please, Mary, put two of them back. They are supporting the roof.

And I say, "Hey, I am looking forward to a mild winter." See, I live in the East, where it snows. That puts a little pressure on the roof. But, we'll see. It looks good.

Then we fixed the floor. Now, I made a little mistake with the floor. You see, we put new wood on half the floor. And half the floor had old wood. And I tried matching stains. But that's very difficult and beyond my expertise.

So I decided to paint the floor. It's a country kitchen. I thought it would look nice. Sturbridge Village Tavern Table Blue. Very pretty.

'Cept – no one told me that the knotholes on fresh wood would bleed. And you have to put something on that so they won't do that. Well, I put down two coats of Tavern Table Blue, three coats of polyurethane, and those little knotholes bled right through. My kitchen floor sort of looks like I have a puppy.

Oh, well. But the really important thing that I learned was that women and men do not approach work the same way. You'd think I know that already. These guys that I hired to build that addition at $30 an hour apiece had a structure about their work.

They would arrive about 8:30 in the morning, walk around the job a little bit, look at what they did yesterday. At 10:15 they would send one of them for coffee and doughnuts. Fifteen miles there, and 15 miles back.

At 12:30, they would have lunch with copious amounts of carbohydrates, which I never saw them spend, and at 4 o'clock they left. That is not the way women work. We don't have the time. We would start at 9 sharp, and work until we got silly.

Now, men attach a certain kind of attitude toward challenges. You know, there's always a part in a construction thing that presents a problem to you. And men sort of look at it and they mumble at it. Mmmmm, mmmm. Mmmmm …

Women like to talk about problems. You know. We talk about it to each other. Or, if no one else is in the room, we talk about it to ourselves. What am I going to do? How am I going to fix this?

Perhaps, if I shim it and all of that stuff, it's not going to work. You better cut a whole new piece of wood. And then when they solve the problem, is there any joy in Mudville? No, they have a different kind of mumble for that. It's sort of macho mumble: Memmmmm, memmmmmmm.

Not women. Women, when we solve a problem, we're overjoyed by it. We would look at each other and go, "Yes."

I did realize a great truth at the end of all of this. The night before the wedding I realized that I had not made a shelf for the microwave. So I ran around the outside of the house to a little pile of wood where we put all of the spare, you know, pieces. And found the right size.

And ran back into the house. And screwed on two L's to it and screwed it up onto the wall. And realized, of course, it's now 11 o'clock at night. And I said to myself, "I've got to paint it." But it won't dry by tomorrow.

So I put the microwave on the shelf. I got out the paint and painted around it. It was then that I understood the fundamental difference. Men like things to be perfect. Women understand the existential nature of the world and only ask it to look good.

Kansas City, Mo.
Granddaughters

AUGUST 19, 1993

I have been having a wonderful experience since we did the Peter, Paul and Mommy II television program.

First place, people stop me in the street and say, "Your granddaughter is gorgeous." And she is. And now she's family. I have two granddaughters.

One needs a theatrical agent, the other needs an exorcist.

The one you didn't see in the television program was busy dismantling the fire hose in the theater.

Wolftrap, Vienna, Va.
Machines, Son-in-Law

AUGUST 24, 1996

Noel Paul's introduction includes Mary's various natures from Blond Bombshell to being a witch. Here, she hit the stage with a witch welcome.

Cackle, cackle, cackle.

Now, do I say things like that about him? I mean, it is true that he has become absolutely obsessed with machines.

You hear it in his music. He is writing songs about machines.

I myself am a Luddite. I know this from the very first time that I used a vacuum cleaner. A profound epiphany came to me ... that there are two different kinds of people in this world.

There's the person who plugs it into the wall, vacuums until they reach the end of the cord, goes backs and unplugs it, finds another receptacle, and continues.

And then, there are the people who plug it into the wall, vacuum, get to the end of the cord and pull. I belong to the latter.

When I first learned how to drive, my mother had a 1939 LaSalle convertible. It was an old car even then. But when you opened up the hood, there was an engine in there with recognizable parts. One morning I went to take the car and the engine went kerloop, kerloop.

So in the movies, you open up the hood. And I got my six-year-old sister to step on the gas and turn the ignition on, and I saw those little sparks jumping. I had taken shop in school. So I went into the house, got a Band-Aid, I put it on the wire, and drove off.

Have you looked in the engine of your car lately?

First place, it's just solid stuff. And when something is wrong with it, you take it to the repair place, they hook it up to a machine, and the machine tells them what's wrong with your machine.

And the repairman goes into his office, opens up his desk, takes out a little thingy about this big, a chip, puts it into your car, and charges you $700.

This is taking the fun out of it. But it's beyond me now. I want an old car, with recognizable parts. You know, it's kind of like guys.

Now my son-in-law, who is a very sweet man who I have been teasing for many, many years, mostly because he is a Republican – someone has to marry them.

He's very nice. But I love to tease him. You know. And when he asked for my daughter's hand in marriage, I said, "Well, I'm losing a daughter, but you are losing your security clearance.

He's big into toys. He works as a computer person, big-time computer person. Worldwide computer person. Fiber optics. Stuff I don't understand. He comes to dinner. He's okay if you give him a machine to fix, you know.

But last summer he bought a plane. He flies. He bought a plane. He was very excited. He bought an antique plane. A 1937 Piper Cub. I was born in 1936. I wasn't thrilled with this label. I said, look darling, can't you just call it a classic aircraft. So he decided to do something that parents often wish they would do but never do.

He went and took a trip with my oldest granddaughter, just the two of them. And they flew across country in this classic aircraft ... and had a fabulous time.

Meanwhile I was touring in the Pacific Northwest. So they were coming up and I was going down. And he called me on the telephone to tell me this incredible story. They landed the aircraft in a little airport outside of Abilene, Texas.

There was one other classic aircraft on the field. And he's describing, "There were these two old codgers on the field."

Now I didn't have the nerve to ask him what an old codger is because I already know what he thinks "antique" is. It's probably somebody 50.

Anyway, one of the gentlemen gets out of his aircraft and starts walking towards Jeff.

"And Jeff is saying to himself ... you know how guys are about their toys ... "Coming to ask me about my 1937 Piper Cub – there are only nine of them in the country in this condition. I'm going to show them the stuff.""

And the guy walks right by him. And goes right to my granddaughter. And says, "Excuse me, but aren't you Mary Travers' granddaughter? So she says, "Why, yes."

And the guy says, "I knew it. I saw the 1937, saw the beautiful little girl, and you" – meaning Jeff – "you must be the Republican."

You can't make this stuff up. My daughter says, I didn't have children for you. I had material for you. Well, you know everything's grist for the mill. Trust Mom if you don't want to hear it in seven states.

Houston, Texas
House in Connecticut

SEPTEMBER 10, 1997

All right, so I am not the best driver in the world.
I knew it was going to come to this. Not quite so soon. I knew one day we were going to be standing on the stage in our walkers and canes.

I just didn't know I was going to be the first one.

Oh, well. I love to listen to Noel sing his computer song. Because you know next to religion – computers become really a compulsion. I mean once they fall in love with those things – everything.

I mean, once upon a time way back in the middle ages – those guys used to read Playboy. Now they read a book, a magazine called Byte. It's not B-I-T-E, it's B-Y-T-E. They've got all these computer books they read. And they're really into it. They are talking about it all the time.

They are talking about upgrading that, putting more stuff into this one, and the merits of that. I hate computers. I find that life is just moving too quick for me. Because everything I want to do - I have to put my glasses on for.

You know I used to be able to memorize people's phone numbers.

That's when they were PLaza 5-6438. You know, that was easy. Now you have to remember the one, the area code, and then these seven digits.

And if that weren't bad enough, now you can call New York, and you may have to use three different area codes depending on whether you are calling Long Island, upstate, or Brooklyn. This is three area codes too many ... which is why I moved to Connecticut. I have one area code there. And if there is another one, it's north of me and I don't care.

I live in Connecticut in a 1740 house, which is very charming, very sweet, and falling apart. And I have had it 31 years. It's the only house that I ever owned. And I never really wanted to buy a house, but my mother ... my mother had a house right up the road from me. And when I was pregnant with my younger daughter, I wanted to rent a house for the summer.

Just for the summer to be close to my mom, to hang out with the baby. It would be nice in the country. So I went looking and I didn't see anything I liked. The real estate agent said, "Oh, there is a house for sale right up the road from your mother."

And I said, "I'm not interested in buying a house." And my mother said, "Let's look."

Twenty minutes later I had bought a house. Well, it was easy. It was really cheap. It was $31,000 for a house and five acres. Gone are those days. And it had a $27,000 mortgage on it already. So you can see for four grand I owned a house.

But then it began. It needed a new oil burner. I knew this because the other one blew up. I used to live in the city. You know, cockroaches were the biggest problem.

Then the septic system went. And then I had to put new sills under one side of the house. Then I discovered that only half of the house had a foundation. You have been there. There is someone clapping madly. I know. You bought this house, right?

You sold it to me! I believe it. And then I found out the neighborhood I had moved into — there were two Democrats — my mother and me. And then it began. The year was 1967. There was an article in *Look* magazine, which no longer exists. There was a magazine called *Look*.

And there was an article about the new, emerging ecology movement. And there was a big, big full-page picture of a young girl sort of like Christina's World sitting on a hill. And she had this huge flag on her lap that was green and white. It looked like the American flag, but it was green and white. I stress this, because when the police came, and told me to take it down, because I was violating section blah, blah, blah of the Flag Code, I kept saying, "But it's green and white."

Then I realized what was really happening here. The neighborhood had discovered that I was not in favor of the Vietnam War. So they naturally assumed, these stupid Republicans, that the green and white flag, which really symbolized Keep America Green... they believed it symbolized something covert.

My mother said maybe you should keep it down. That's when the septic system went. And I said to her, Mom, if I really thought something bad would happen, I'd fly the Viet Cong flag and collect the insurance.

However — I thought about it for maybe a moment or two about why the town is a little sensitive. And then the children said, "Mom, put it back. Show them what you are made of." Right. So it went back!

About three months later, my children decided to have a fair — a pin-the-tale-on-the-donkey, a throw-the-football-through-the-tire, and a pet show. Bring your turtles and your birds. The kids, knowing I'm a guilty kind of mother, as all working mothers are, bamboozled me into making homemade doughnuts.

So there I was at 6 o'clock in the morning of the fair making doughnuts and burning my fingers when I heard this bang, bang, bang outside my window. In my Wesson Oil-stained nightgown, I went to the door. Looking out, I saw a state trooper banging signs into the road – "No Parking."

In Redding, Connecticut, the road I live on, is not really wide enough for two cars. Much less anybody parking on a shoulder, of which there isn't any. Just sort of goes up on either side. And my parking area fits three cars. Hardly a space big enough for a Ferris wheel, which is what the state trooper thought I was going to have.

So I call the first selectman, that's the mayor in New England. And I said, "Jesse," (mind you, it's now 6:30 in the morning, but you figure what the heck, right? His policeman was making noise. I can wake him up. After all, I didn't vote for him.)

"Jesse, what is the state trooper out here doing?" And he said, "Well, you're having a fair, aren't you?"

And I said, "No, no, the children are having this little lemonade stand, sell mommy's bad doughnuts.

"Well, you're supposed to get a permit."

I said, "A permit? What kind of fair do you think I am having?"

"Well, you're supposed to get a permit."

"Well, Jesse, it's just the kids. They are ten, seven and five. What is this?"

"Well, we never know what you people will do next."

So this is the little town. There's no reason why I told you this story. I just thought it was an interesting story you had never heard before. Why not?

You know they are still talking about the flag! Lo, these many years later. That's all right. Now they have to abide by all of those ecology rules. ... It's true, though. It's all true. I never make things up. It's because my mother used to say to me when I was younger – "Mary, you really don't lie well. Best stick to the truth."

Ohhhhhhh, I've been pierced to the soul. Well, we're only beginners when it comes to you guys. Let's put it this way. If you're referring to politicians, most of them avoid the truth on both sides of the aisle.

Anyhow, I don't know what launched me off into that. I guess part of it was thinking about all of this reaction to computers and the fact that I have to dial my telephone with my glasses on, or call my daughter to remind me how to work the VCR because I can never remember.

And besides, why do they design those things with all of these black ... the whole surface is black. And it's smooth. All the little things you push. They are all smooth. I want them to be color-coded.

You know, made by Mattel. One of the toy companies should design the front of them so I can see it. So in thinking about all of this rush to the 21st century, I'm not interested in the 21st century. I'm not going to spend a lot of time in it.

When I was looking for songs this summer, I found a song that was very much a part of reflecting on some of the great people of the 20th century. What an incredible century we've been living through. What wonderful people.

I sure hope that the 21st century will have some heroes and heroines as good as the ones we've had in this generation.

San Diego, Calif.
Getting Old

JULY 30, 1999

There are a lot of nice things about getting old.

And there are a lot of things that aren't so nice.

151

I watch fashions and I see now that tie-dye is back. But … I'm not going to wear go-go boots. Forget that. Once was enough.

Short skirts – in another life. I don't have the thighs for it anymore. So there are some things that are not going to come back in my closet.

I'm not wearing glasses as an affectation. Although, God knows, in the Sixties we did. Remember the Jackie O glasses? Huge. They were great. I am wearing them now because I am developing a little cataract in one eye, and it's not, the doctor said, ripe enough to do anything about it.

Now that would be okay, because I am so near-sighted in that eye that I can't see out of it anyway. But when the lights are really bright, it makes me sneeze. Something about the light refracting off this little film that I am developing makes me sneeze.

Now I have to tell you – if you are in the middle of "Leaving on a Jet Plane," you don't want to sneeze. So I decided I would try shades and see if that helped. I think it's going to be okay. It's still bright though.

Anyway, so things are happening, things are changing. And I'm finding that all of this excitement about entering the 21st century and millennium madness is just so boring. It's boring. First place I'm not upset about the new millennium or even interested in it since I am not planning on spending a great deal of time in it. They'll have to do most of it without me.

And the other thing about the new millennium is that I'm really not sure where it's going because all I see is all this technology, most of which I can't operate. I mean the phone, I loved it, when it was black and chunky, and it sat on the hall table. No one ever asked where it was. I mean, the Pottery Barn has brought it back.

I mean, I live in a little town, where we used to just have five-digit phone numbers. Then they had to go from rotary to push button. Now we have to have the full seven. I can never remember them. I could remember seven when it was PLaza 3, something, something, something, something. But now we have a lot of numbers to remember. The phone itself, I have to put my glasses on to make a phone call. I can't see those little numbers. On top of that, they are so small that you really have to be careful because your finger is fatter than the thing you push.

And everybody's got a cell phone. I find it appalling. You go into a restaurant where you know you are going to spend a great deal of money and there's someone at the next table having a telephone conversation. I don't want to hear it! I want to hear mmm, the veal is marvelous. That's what I want to hear.

We were touring in Australia last year. They are really crazy about cellular phones. I was trying on clothes and I heard this woman talking to herself. Then I heard tinkle, tinkle, tinkle – and she's still talking. Then I realized she was on the phone.

Now, come on – this is carrying things too far. It's just gone too far for me. I mean, I can't operate my television set anymore. Well, it has this remote thing, God forbid, we should get up and change channels.

You know the people who surf, who are constantly clicking, if they had to get up, they would settle on a show and watch it. And then, I have to look where the little thing is – up or down. Because one day I hit something, and the entire screen went blue. It said menu, menu, menu, menu. I had to call long-distance to one of my kids to find out how to get the hell out of it.

I am technologically challenged. I understand this. Absolutely. I'm the kind of person when it doesn't work, I kick it. Peter had a little tape recorder one day, and it wouldn't work in rehearsal.

He said, "Oh gee, it's not working." I said, "Well, what did you do with it?"

He said, "I dropped it." I said, "Give it to me."

And he gave it to me, and I dropped it. It worked fine.

Ah, well. What's going to happen, though, when I'm a little old lady? Well, I'll never be little. But I will be an old lady. You know, and I don't know how to operate anything.

I saw this thing on television the other day. They were talking about a fridge that had a screen built in to the door. And it read the bar codes on your food. So if you reached in and got a quart of milk, and it was not full, you could run it across this bar code, and it would make a grocery list for you. And then it would call the grocer.

Now it sounded very interesting. Except I don't know where the person who is buying this fridge lives. But I don't think the Safeway is going to take my order over the telephone. It's just not going to happen.

It's sort of bizarre. What's going to happen is I'm going to have to hire some high school student to come over after school and run all the machines in my house. That's going to be the wave of the future for those of us who are challenged.

I want to go back to a simpler time. When you opened up the hood of your car, and you could recognize the stuff down there. My car didn't work the other day. I opened up the hood. And you know the thing that used to look like an octopus with these little legs coming out. It's not there anymore. Where is it? It's gone.

In its place is some little chip thing. Now I had a car once that had a little problem with that thing, because the wire had kind of worn down and it was grounding on the engine block. Right? Okay? So I ran in the house and got a Band-Aid and put it on the wire. The car worked fine.

Now my car doesn't work. I have to have it put on a flatbed and dragged over to the filling station. God forbid that they should hook up something to it. And then the guy opens up the hood, drags over a little box on wheels, attaches something to my car, and his computer talks to my computer. And his computer says, "Where does it hurt, honey?"

And my computer tells him. And then he puts a new chip in and charges me $600. I liked the Band-Aid better.

CHAPTER 8

♂he ♂ꞁadio ꞁears

*Mary's radio show, "Mary Travers & Friends," was produced for broadcast on
AOR (Album Oriented Rock) stations and syndicated through Westwood One
in the 1975. The show aired on Sunday nights on hundreds of stations across
the country.*

*Many of the performers were established, but a number of them were
just starting out. Mary interviewed musical artists such as Bob Dylan
Richie Havens, Melissa Manchester, Renaissance, New Riders of the Purple
Sage, LaBelle, Billy Joel, Janis Ian, Neil Sedaka, Barry Manilow,
Dory Previn, Jerry Garcia of the Grateful Dead, and Harry Chapin,
among others.*

*Shelley Belusar was Mary's tour manager when she was a solo, was
PPM's tour manager for more than 30 years, and was the maid of honor at
Mary's wedding to Ethan Robbins. She recalls the radio years with warm
smiles and laughs:*

When I first met Mary, she was married to Jerry Taylor, the
publisher of National Lampoon magazine. What a fun place to be.
They had a recording studio on Madison Avenue and had many creative
people who were working on a show called "Lemmings" that was to be
performed at the Village Gate.

On the air in New York in 1975. (AP Photo/Suzanne Vlamis)

Mary was given an office right across from the recording studio when they developed her radio show. To get to our office we had to pass in front of several other offices, one in particular located in the corner of the building. I would look in and see John Belushi and Judy, who he later married, Christopher Guest, Chevy Chase sitting on the floor working out comedy routines for "Lemmings." Gilda Radner would stop in to visit. This, of course was pre-SNL [Saturday Night Live], but it was where the show originated. Lorne Michaels was also working for the National Lampoon Magazine at the time.

We had to travel to the West Coast to do Bob Dylan and Harry Nilsson. I should say the first two attempts to interview Bob Dylan were in New York – once upstairs on the third floor of Mary's brownstone – and that didn't work because of the ambient noise from the street. The second time was in a recording studio, which would have been fine except Mick Jagger and the Stones were in the next studio and everyone had more interest in sitting in the control booth watching them.

Finally, we flew to L.A. for the third and last attempt of trying to get enough coherent and audible sentences without extraneous noise to complete the interview. When it was done, the radio engineer certainly had his job cut out to piece as much together as he could to fill the time slot. It aired in the first broadcast of the show.

Interview With Bob Dylan

MARY: Hi, this is Mary Travers. And welcome to *Mary Travers and Friends*. My very special friend today is Bob Dylan. Today we are going to talk about music and some of the music Bob Dylan has liked and some of the music that I have liked over the years. And some names and some singers that may be unfamiliar to some of you listening. One of their names, when we were going through the records, is a guy named Peter LaFarge. When did you first meet Peter?

DYLAN: I met Peter in 1960.

MARY: At Newport?

DYLAN: In New York. I used to hang around in the same place.

MARY: I think it was Café Wha? I remember that. I think Peter, Paul and Mary did one or two turns. There's a song on Peter's album called "I'll Bring You Flowers," which is kind of a silly song. But a fun song.

MARY: Well, I am a little bit nervous. I've never done this before. It's the first time I have been on this end of the microphone. I'm usually on your end. I'm usually being interviewed, not interviewing.

DYLAN: Well, let me interview you.

MARY: Well, sure. Terrific. I would prefer to be on the other side.

DYLAN: Okay. In the last group you were in, Peter, Paul and Albert [an inside joke about manager Albert Grossman who managed PP&M and Bob Dylan], what happened to Peter? You went one way, Peter went one way. And Paul went another way.

MARY: Well, Paul went and got religion.

DYLAN: He was always religious.

MARY: He came from the Midwest, a WASP version of your background. Small town. Suburbs. Well, he was more suburbs, suburbs of Detroit. A little bit bigger than Hibbing, where you originated from. So that I suppose the whole renaissance of religion was not so strange. Peter's got a band, a pretty good band. And he's singing around and working as a solo.

DYLAN: Do you think you'll ever get back together?

MARY: Never, never, never ... *never*! I don't think so. We are very different people. [Peter, Paul and Mary reunited in 1978.]

DYLAN: Well, why did you ever get together in the first place?

MARY: 'Cause we weren't so different – then. None of us were that much different then. We were all – you, myself, very young, hanging out in the Gaslight. Bushy-tailed, bright-eyed, wanting to cure the world. Or, at least, sing about it.

DYLAN: Folks were laughing their socks off.

MARY: Peter wrote a lot of good songs. You wrote a lot of good songs. There were a lot of good songs being written.

DYLAN: When you sing, do you still do that thing with your hair?

MARY: Yes, because it still gets in my face. I guess that was known as a mannerism of mine.

DYLAN: Yes.

MARY: I never did it on purpose. I never realized I did it until ...

DYLAN: Do you do it now?

MARY: Subconsciously, I was never the last of the graceful ladies.

DYLAN: You were like a horse.

MARY: Well, it's a little glumpy.

DYLAN: Well, you were really good, though, when you were singing at the Gaslight.

MARY: I was so terrified. I used to shake. I mean, everything shook. Legs shook, hands shook.

DYLAN: That was all a part of it. You never knew you did all that shaking?

MARY: No, I was just scared.

DYLAN: I thought that was part of the act, when you were shaking.

MARY: Oh, did you? No, it wasn't part of the act. That was just called terror.

Do you find yourself — is it funny to be a parent, when you still feel like you are not grown up? Do you ever think you feel like you are grown up?

DYLAN: It's grown up to what?

MARY: I don't know.

DYLAN: How can you be grown up?

MARY: I don't think it is something to aspire to.

DYLAN: No. It's like death.

MARY: Grown up is finished?

DYLAN: Yeah. It's all over.

MARY: Do you have an image —some kind of responsible ...

DYLAN: You grow up and you don't feel anymore.

MARY: But, that shouldn't be what grown up is.

DYLAN: Well, grown up isn't really a real word. What does that mean?

MARY: It's a concept, I think.

DYLAN: That's for people who want to stifle other people. Mature, grown-up words. It's just because when someone else has to do something, they don't want you to have something that they can't have.

MARY: Yes.

DYLAN: Who's really grown up – is Nixon grown up?

MARY: I don't think so.

DYLAN: Who's like a parent that you look up to? Who was a perfect parent? I mean, is there such a thing?

MARY: Gregory Peck?

DYLAN: Gregory Peck, wow!

MARY: Hank Fonda?

DYLAN: Hank Snow? Hank Fonda – now he's got some kids. Would you call him a perfect parent? Grown up? Would you call him grown up?

MARY: Ah, no. Is Picasso…?

DYLAN: There you go.

MARY: Now he was … maybe, he was a grown-up. But in a good sense. But there is no such thing as a perfect parent?

DYLAN: Well, is there such a thing as a grown up?

MARY: Maybe, there isn't. Maybe we should just scrap the whole bloody term to begin with. But, why do we keep it as a culture [where] people aspire to that concept?

DYLAN: Because the culture is false. It's not aspiring at all.

MARY: Do you think that this culture is disintegrating?

DYLAN: No, I don't think there is anything to disintegrate.

MARY: Well, okay.

DYLAN: Really. What is there to disintegrate?

MARY: Well, there is a concept that it was once – at one time we moved forward, we had frontiers.

DYLAN: Frontiers …

MARY: And then, we stopped moving when we had frontiers and started building upwards.

DYLAN: Frontiers.

MARY: You like that word?

DYLAN: Back tiers and front tiers – boy, I don't know if those are real concepts, I mean, this country was here from 6,000 years ago – I mean, what is this "frontiers" that all of a sudden came into being in the last 50, 60, 200 years?

MARY: Our frontiers.

DYLAN: That is a tremendous amount of egotism, you know.

MARY: Absolutely. But mankind has been viewed with egotism for as long as he's been here.

DYLAN: I mean, Peter was such a great artist. Because he just kept pushing all the time.

MARY: Which Peter?

DYLAN: This Peter?

MARY: Pete Seeger?

DYLAN: Well, him, too. But Peter LaFarge. He just kept pushing all of the time. He was never there. He just kept pushing – all the time. He was just going further and further. Eventually, it killed him. In this life, anyway. But you can't have any frontiers. It's endless.

MARY: That's like saying in a way that you can't have any goals.

DYLAN: Well, you can't.

MARY: To me, a goal is limiting. Sooner or later you have to reach it. It's like growing up.

DYLAN: Having a goal is like putting a fence up. Experience really takes place right in there. I mean, how much of a day do you really experience? You know, when you go out to buy a quart of milk, do you really experience that? Going out to buy a quart of milk? That's a waste of time, really. Or – is there really anything that's a waste of time?

MARY: Yes, I believe there is such a thing as a waste of time. But I don't think you have to waste the time.

DYLAN: But if you are driving through Connecticut for two hours – are you experiencing that?

161

MARY: Well, it depends if I take the scenic route. I experience something.

DYLAN: Well, you can't drive and look at the same time.

MARY: No, I mean there are levels of awareness. You can experience …

DYLAN: You can be a little bit of weird.

MARY: Okay, it depends on what you are looking for. When I am riding a horse, I am not only looking at the horizon line, but I'm also looking at the ground. Because if I lead my horse into a gopher hole, we can both break our neck. It is important for me to look at the ground. In the process of looking at the ground, I also see many of the things I would not normally see. Now that is a certain level of awareness.

DYLAN: Do you experience those things?

MARY: Yes.

DYLAN: Like what other things.

MARY: It's a very mixed experience.

DYLAN: Bushes, trees …

MARY: Bushes, trees, bee's holes, shells, things on the ground, garbage, cigarette packs, jack rabbits, life. You can see a lot. Except when people … except in New York when people avoid poop. But most people don't look at the ground where they walk. But I think it depends on the person. A lot of people walk around like zombies. How much of the time are you aware? Are you fighting to stay awake?

DYLAN: Yes, it's a continuous battle. I mean I just walked over here from Sixth Avenue and something, and boy, I was dead the whole way. I was lucky I didn't get murdered by a car. I didn't see anything. I just walked straight over here. I knew I was going to be here, so … I mean, if I had experienced anything, I wouldn't have gotten here.

MARY: You would have turned away?

DYLAN: I wouldn't know where I was. I would never have showed up.

MARY: If something had happened?

DYLAN: Yes.

MARY: Odetta. I've never known anybody who hung themselves.

DYLAN: Oh, really. Never knew that crowd?

MARY: No, no. Survival. I belong to that class.

DYLAN: Well, Van Gogh. Look at Van Gogh. I mean, you can't say that Van Gogh didn't survive.

MARY: Want to talk about survival? What it is? Because there are lots of different kinds.

DYLAN: How many different kinds of survival are there?

MARY: Depends.

DYLAN: Let's talk about ...

MARY: Depends on how existential you want to get. What has meaning?

DYLAN: Okay, well, let's decide that – make sure we are both talking about the same thing.

MARY: What has meaning?

DYLAN: What has meaning? Time has meaning. What else has meaning? Nothing.

MARY: The dinosaur was here a lot longer than we've been here.

DYLAN: Time killed him.

MARY: Does he still have meaning?

DYLAN: Time has meaning. What about the dinosaurs?

MARY: Yes, but it's all different kinds of time.

DYLAN: Time is the same thing. Time is ... there aren't different kinds of time. There's one time.

MARY: Do you feel time? Do you feel the pressure of time?

DYLAN: Oh, boy. Yes.

MARY: Sometimes, I don't feel like I have enough time.

DYLAN: Well, everybody's got to feel that way.

MARY: There are times when I feel that I want to say something, and I know that part of it I have to learn how to say. And part of it hasn't occurred to me yet. Part of it is going to, and it's all pending, and I feel the push by time, see? You have to formulate, consolidate, you have to be able to express and say it, and figure out. Because to perform for me has a certain amount of pressure behind it. When it's time to go on, it is time to go on.

DYLAN: I have no idea why I am performing. No idea, whatsoever. I don't even care.

MARY: You are just enjoying it?

DYLAN: If that's the word ...

MARY: Experiencing it?

DYLAN: Experiencing it, yes. I always have done it. It's not that I am doing anything new.

MARY: Well, it's new in the sense that it's an exposure to yourself, that you have spent a lot of years not doing.

DYLAN: It's illusion, though.

MARY: I don't know how much illusion it was at Madison Square Garden.

DYLAN: All illusion.

MARY: In what sense?

DYLAN: You know, in every sense. In the real sense of the word, in reality, it's illusion.

MARY: I don't understand it. See, for me, I know when I listen to a record sometimes ...

DYLAN: That's false.

MARY: That's an engineer's construction, his dream. You go in and lay your track.

DYLAN: These are good records. There is very little illusion to them. They are real. They are an environment type of thing. You put them on and imagine. They leave something for you to imagine.

MARY: They are more like radio, as opposed to television.

DYLAN: Radio is much better than television, isn't it?

MARY: I remember your friend Barry Feinstein once said ...

DYLAN: Your friend ...

MARY: Our friend ... that he hated to shoot in color because it just faked you out. Spatial relationships, what the balance of the picture was, or was there anything in the picture?

DYLAN: He did great color photos of the tour. Great color photos. As great as they could be. And the approach with the color was really light. I mean they just were not real. His black and white photos are real.

MARY: Color fakes you out.

DYLAN: The color isn't real color. What in this room is real color? You can go to a movie and see real color.

MARY: But getting back to the music, when it happens in a performance, it's more real to me. Why people went might have been why.

MARY: We're here in the studio with Bob and there are a lot of good musical questions to talk about. First, I'd like to talk a little bit about some of the folks that the two of us were listening to in the early '60s. People like Woody Guthrie, and let's open if we may with a song you wrote about Woody Guthrie.

MARY: And now let's play the real Woody Guthrie. Shall we?

■

MARY: What about Guthrie? Did you ever meet him?

DYLAN: Yes, I did.

MARY: Was he sick then?

Taking a smoke break with Bob Dylan and Donovan at the Newport Folk
Festival in the summer of 1965 (Photo by David Gahr/Getty Images).

DYLAN: He was sick then. He was in his prime time, I guess. When
         I met him, he was pretty laid up, but he was alive and
         alert. I made many visits out to see him in the hospital.
MARY: Yes, he had Huntington's disease.
DYLAN: A shaky thing, you know.
MARY: This is Mary Travers and I'll be right back after this
         message with Bob Dylan.

■

MARY: You've done an album that isn't released yet called "The
         Basement Tapes." Want to tell me about that?
DYLAN: That was recorded in '66, '67 up in Woodstock before
         Woodstock. Before the big Woodstock Festival. Before
         Woodstock was discovered, exploited. We were just all up
         there drying out.

MARY: You and the band?

DYLAN: Yeah, members of The Band and various other people were up there making music and planting gardens and just watching time go by. So in the meantime, we made this record. Actually, it wasn't a record – it was just songs where we had come to this basement and recorded out in the woods. That's basically it, really. The record's been exposed throughout the year, so someone mentioned it was a good idea to put it out so people could hear it in its entirety. And that's exactly what we were doing up there in those years. It'll be out shortly.

MARY: We can play a track off of it?

DYLAN: We can play all of the tracks.

MARY: We'll play one track now and some more later.

MARY: Do you think that that period was a good period to hang out and kind of relax and get back to what music was about for you?

DYLAN: For me ...

MARY: In the sense that when you are on tour and you are working hard, I know I find – I write poetry, I don't write songs. I find it very difficult to write on the road. Between getting on and off a plane and bad food, and staying at the Holiday Inn, it leaves you – it saps you of the kind of contemplative time you need to sit around and really think. And you also don't play so much together.

DYLAN: Yeah, well, these songs basically on the tape were written in five or ten minutes. We had come off of a ferocious tour – Australia and Europe, England. And we needed some time to let it all – let the dust settle. Settle so the waves could come in.

MARY: Well, I think a lot of people go through periods like that. If you forget how to have fun with music, you have destroyed it for yourself. And, I think, unfortunately, that's what heavy touring often does to us all. You know, it becomes a job.

DYLAN: It becomes a business.

MARY: Perhaps that is the kind of genesis of *The Basement Tapes*. It's to go back and have fun with music. Let's play another track from that.

MARY: In a sense, this is a kind of retrospective album for you. And you've had some funny albums. I take that back. Most people do albums because you have to do X number of albums a year. And then when you get tired, or I get tired, and it's happened to me, too, you throw out a "Best Of" and kind of hang around and try to figure out what it is that you really want to say musically.

DYLAN: Musically, I just play and whatever comes out, comes out. I don't plan albums. All that pressure is off. I don't have to go in and make an album every six months. I don't think of it that way. I just continue to play my guitar. If there is a song to be sung ... in my heart to do, I'll do it.

MARY: Let's maybe go back to Guthrie and see if we can't explore that a little more. He obviously had a great affect on your music and on a great many writers in that period. You can see his influence even now. His talking blues form is very viable and will always be a viable form of saying something. And he wrote songs like *Pastures and Plenty* and *This Land is Your Land* – songs that most people know. And many songs that are not as familiar. But he was also a very social writer and cared very much and came from a time when many artists were very involved in caring about the country and what was happening to it. And I suppose Peter, Paul and Mary and Pete Seeger and the Weavers and yourself, even, were caught up in that social commentary way of viewing the world as we saw it at that time. There were certainly a lot of your songs like that. Do you feel that that's not a reasonable position to take now or is it just that you are caring about other things?

DYLAN: No, it's a very reasonable position to take now. It's just hard to be specific about what we are even talking about here. Let alone, try to write a song, do a play, or make some kind of art form out of these big situations which are happening in the world, which are happening so fast now from day to day. It's, like, you know they are rolling over too fast to keep your finger or your eye on them. Whereas, back then, when Woody was doing all his writing, you know things, communications and the media weren't so powerful.

MARY: And it also took longer to get something changed.

DYLAN: Longer to get anywhere. It took longer to get from here to there.

MARY: I guess what you are saying really is that it presents a special kind of problem for people who write that kind of material.

DYLAN: Well, it's getting to be confusing. If you want to write topical songs, it's hard to find the frontier.

MARY: You wrote a lot of good topical songs.

DYLAN: I wrote those songs before it was happening. And before it's happening, and you do it, before everybody is on your case. Everybody gets on your case, you don't want to do it anymore. It's like anything else, people tell you what to do. It's discouraging.

MARY: Yes, I noticed …

DYLAN: You are just writing over the same ground.

MARY: You've said it. And I think you have to say, "The times, they are a changing."

DYLAN: Say it again, say it again. That's what they want.

MARY: Yeah, what they want.

MARY: Did you ever meet Nina Simone?

DYLAN: I met her at a table once somewhere, at a club.

MARY: She did a couple of your tunes. And well, I thought.

DYLAN: Roberta Flack did *Just Like a Woman* – but she got the words wrong.

MARY: She changed the words.

DYLAN: I don't think she changed them – she got them wrong.

MARY: Nina Simone did *Just Like a Woman* as well. I think she makes a lyric change there.

DYLAN: Personally, I don't know why anyone would want to do that song except me.

MARY: Richie Havens did it.

DYLAN: With Richie, it made sense coming from Richie.

MARY: Let's play a little Richie. I love him as a musician, I love his work, I love him as a human being.

DYLAN: He's like a king.

MARY: Okay, let's talk about the present, because we can't talk about the future ... since it doesn't exist yet. And the future right now is this ...

DYLAN: The present exists, the past exists, the future exists. It all exists.

MARY: How do you see the future as existing?

DYLAN: It exists as part of the present.

MARY: In the sense that ...

DYLAN: It's connected. It just depends on how far you want to set yourself up. I think you could be very limited. The Zen philosophy – you just live in the present. But that's more complicated than meets the eye or meets the ear. But it's all the same. The past, the present, the future.

MARY: Historically, it would seem so.

DYLAN: You know we may be crossing the line here .... I don't know if we are the right people ...

MARY: We are the right people ...

DYLAN: Maybe you should be talking about that with someone else. Or neither one of us should be talking about it.

MARY: Okay. That's fine. Those questions are philosophical questions. This program really isn't about philosophy. It's about music ... there is a lot of philosophy in music. And a lot in yours, which is self-evident.

DYLAN: That philosophy in my music is accidental. None of it is really preconceived.

MARY: Well, now, when you say preconceived – I know when I write something, write a poem, I don't sit around all day saying, "I'd like to write a poem about flowers, or children, or caring about people." I don't think about what it is I am going to write about. When you feel like writing, you sit down and out something pops. But it doesn't mean that you haven't been thinking about it. It means you haven't been consciously thinking about it.

DYLAN: Well, that's thinking. It gets back to thinking again. Most of it has more to do with feeling than thinking.

MARY: Okay.

DYLAN: When I get to thinking, I'm usually in some kind of trouble.

MARY: Well, feeling is often – if you can trust your feelings and you'll probably be in better shape. Is it more truthful?

DYLAN: Oh, yeah. It comes out to mutual trust.

MARY: Yes, always. On *Blood on the Tracks,* I have to tell you that, needless to say, I loved the album. I really enjoyed the album. It was funny when we had talked before, we talked about the recording processes. And how when they get very complex, much of the truth of the piece of music is lost. It becomes something else. And, one of the things I enjoyed about *Blood on the Tracks* was that it was very simple.

DYLAN: Well, that's the way things are – they are basically very simple. Well, a lot of people told me they enjoyed the album. It's hard for me to relate to that. People are enjoying the type of pain.

MARY: It is a painful album. Well, perhaps maybe the word "enjoy" is the wrong word. Maybe a better word is to say that you are moved by the album. There were things I could relate to in the album that made sense to me. You made sense to me on that album. I felt that it was much more, for me, it was much more first-person as opposed to third-person.

DYLAN: Well, it makes it more clearly defined, but it still doesn't necessarily make it any better – because you can do it second-, third-, fourth-person – it's all the same. I know what you mean, though.

MARY: Now let's play *If You See Her, Say Hello*. I think that is a very beautiful song.

DYLAN: Very pertinent.

MARY: For me, that was a very poignant song. And a very sad song. But, together, I think one of the things I like about your work is when you are feeling bad, it isn't self-pity bad. It's just, I don't feel good.

DYLAN: When you are feeling down, you are feeling up.

MARY: Well, you are feeling something. And that's the positive as opposed to feeling destroyed by it.

DYLAN: Do you write songs?

MARY: No. I'm writing a book. I write a lot of poetry. But somehow I have never been able to figure out how to make poems into songs. It really seems to be a different way of writing.

DYLAN: Yes, it's confining. Writing songs.

MARY: Well, poetry seems to give you a bigger canvas to play with, and you don't have to explain it the same way. Songs seem to have to be understandable. Somehow in a poem you can ramble and deal with several thoughts. And not have to necessarily connect the images. I know a song of yours that I think was mostly poem is *A Hard Rain's a-Gonna Fall*. Because it really wasn't a song, it was a series of images. And when you see it on a piece of paper, it really looked like a poem.

DYLAN: Play Leon's version.

MARY: Okay.

MARY: The *In Concert* album that you did with The Band on the last tour was incredible. A piece of business for someone doesn't do a lot of concerts. You sure made up for it with that tour. I'd like to play something off of that album. Was there something that you felt went well?

DYLAN: I could play *All Along the Watchtower*.

MARY: Let's finish up with a track from *The Basement Tapes*.

DYLAN: Okay. *Apple Suckling Tree*.

MARY: Okay, we'll finish with that.

Interview With Jerry Garcia

MARY: How did you, for instance, you were very involved in the drug culture, which necessitates that you were advocating something that could do possible harm.

GARCIA: I've never been into telling anybody that it's good one way or another. If anything, there are things that you can definitely say are bad. Actually, you can make those kinds of statements. I'm not into making those statements really. I think that the whole question of stuff like, well, for us, the thing of responsibility in the press and in the straight world, the drugs have always been related to us on our whole trip. For me, I don't think anybody should tell anybody what they can do to themself. One way or another, for whatever reason, on that level I am an anarchist in the extreme. I say no laws – don't have any laws about what anybody does to themself.

MARY: There is a kind of feeling of a personal existentialism.

GARCIA: That's the way I feel about it personally. That's my attitude. But I'm not into selling that as a viewpoint. That's my own viewpoint.

MARY: Unfortunately, the moment that you become public, you are loaded with responsibility.

GARCIA: Right.

MARY: Some of which you would like to see not happen.

GARCIA: I feel that my real responsibility is to the audience in the now. When you are on stage and you are there in the now, in this moment … your real responsibility, and I have been conscious, for example, our audience does get high, whether we tell them to or not. Whether we ask them to or not. No matter what, they get high. So I have a responsibility to try to not injure anybody on the psychic level – for there is a danger in doing that when you have the super, rock-and-roll amazing experience, which is large and full of energy. It's possible to go off in weird directions on that level. To scare people. Like if you see somebody on the street hurt. In that moment, your responsibility isn't your ideas, it's whether you get out and help them. You do something to help them right at that moment. And that's where it is real.

MARY: Your object is not to brutalize.

GARCIA: Or to sermonize. When the Grateful Dead plays, I don't
          even talk to the audience or say stuff to them. Because
          I am that paranoid about the power. I wouldn't want to
          do anything, I wouldn't want to touch that. I am real
          conscious of that stuff. It's already very far out to be playing
          to 15,000 people or 20,000 people, or 30,000 people, or
          60,000, or 70,000. That puts you through changes like
          crazy. Going out there.

MARY: Trying to make one person out of 20,000 is difficult.

GARCIA: It is. It's heavy-duty stuff. I really don't want to blow it
          on that level. I certainly don't want to take the attitude of
          addressing that consciousness with my own little self.

MARY: Well, what about Altamont? [Where a member of the
          audience was stabbed to death at a Rolling Stones concert.]

GARCIA: Well, I was there. I saw it happening and stuff like that.
          And it was as shocking to me as it was to anybody. But
          you know, there was only one of those. There only has
          to be one like that. There only has to be one heavy-
          duty one to scare everybody. And that's the lesson. It's
          hard for me to make judgments about that stuff because
          the results haven't really been seen yet. Altamont did a
          lot toward making it difficult to have large groups of
          people get together.

MARY: Sure.

GARCIA: It virtually killed something that we were very much
          into, which was free music. So it has been weird for us to
          see free music, which started out as such a good, giving
          gesture, a good trip for everybody, to turn into murder.
          That's part of what's happening in America. America has
          that as a possibility — it has those assassinations, it has that
          violence, that stuff, in there.

MARY: It is the ambivalent — it contains both the American dream and that sense of anarchistic violence, frontier-bred violence. And both of those smack dab in the same place.

GARCIA: For me, the experience of Altamont, that's the thing I can relate to, rather than the report — was the experience of it. After it was over, I was amazed to hear that only one person was killed there. I was amazed to hear how few people died there. Because I thought they were dropping like flies. I thought it was total murder. Total mayhem everywhere. It was so psychically damaging, you know what I mean? God. It was supposed to happen. It had to happen. I think that maybe, on the level of responsibility, it's dangerous to be someone like the Rolling Stones, I would think. At those days, I think it was a dangerous thing to be talking about sadism in your sex life, that the Rolling Stones' lyrics had in that innocent level. That was it coming to life.

GARCIA: That was a result of having that as a message. That was the thing if you are putting that out as your lyric — if you are being weird, and you put it out, it comes back to you on some level. You don't get off free, certainly. I just think that eventually everybody who is performing has to deal with that. It's all show biz, which is all mysterious to me in terms of why do people do what they do? And why are other people entertained by it? Things that I am dealing with are much simpler.

MARY: If I were to explain it, as best as I could explain it, is that we are all in a fantasy-world business.

GARCIA: Oh, for sure.

MARY: I have heard many versions about playing high. Do you think being high made the music better?

GARCIA: No, I don't. Well, no, I don't. I think that being high certainly made it something else, besides just music.

MARY: Made it a different kind of experience.

GARCIA: Then the notes would become feelings. It's a whole different experience. The thoughts ...

MARY: Was it just for you a different experience? Or could it transcend itself to the audience?

GARCIA: In those days, our audience wasn't an audience in the concert sense. Our audience was all dancing. And they were all high, too, during this formative period. So the relationship between us and the audience has got to be ... the fact that we were the band at that time didn't mean anything to anybody because we had never made any records. We were just there supplying music at a party. It just sort of evolved into the rock and roll. The Palace trip that Bill Graham sort of took over the idea. LSD became illegal. We all became outlaws. But by that time, we really had a good audience and a good scene going playing just these concerts on the weekends. And by that time it turned into a concert scene.

GARCIA: We no longer had to deal with the clubs. We could concentrate completely on whatever we wanted to do musically. When I was really high in those days, it was a whole different category of events – the guitar would be rubber, the strings would be spider webs, and the whole thing would be this living, breathing thing. And the question of intonation and all of those normal musical things that you think about as a musician, would suddenly be so arbitrary that you wouldn't even develop an opinion about it, or whether you were even in tune or not. So that the experience of playing was something completely different.

GARCIA: But the ideas. You would take back with you to normal life or to the daily routine when you were fiddling with your instrument – back in the normal world, and say, yeah, I remember that there was something about this that suggested something at the time, but I wasn't able to execute it or really deal with it adequately, but now I can sort of bring it back to chunks of new combinations, new syntheses. That's what it really has to do with – the idea of really developing a larger understanding of the vast capacity of the mind. I think drugs are neat for that. But I wouldn't recommend that anyone try to do anything that they felt was critical or important – I don't think that's where they are at. You don't get better, you just get high. You still have to practice if you want to play well. You practice as many hours a day as whatever.

MARY: You still have to put something in the computer.

GARCIA: Yes, that's it – you must. And the more things that you can get into it, that's better. For me, I've always listened to a lot of different kinds of music. So if I hallucinated and suddenly played my guitar and suddenly heard what sounded like an orchestra, or something like that, it would be new stuff to relate it to. Or, far out, the electric guitar is a little bit like French horns with open bells or a glockenspiel. Or you start to see those kinds of things happening.

MARY: You're making a film.

GARCIA: Yes.

MARY: Why are you making the film?

GARCIA: Well, we started out, the film started out as being part of an idea – how could we give the audience "us," without having to send our bodies around. So the idea was if we could capture one really good performance, maybe we would have something like that. Since then the movie has transcended it. But that's the thing that got us into it. It was another way to go. And maybe we could send this movie to places people wouldn't go if there was a security trip. We could have a really good sound system. It was one of the possibilities.

MARY: Then it became like ...

GARCIA: Now it's a movie. It has its own thing, and it's starting to develop a mind and life of its own.

MARY: And I wish that were television, this one moment, because the expression on your face ... as if you have discovered just a wonderful, new toy. It isn't even a Cheshire smile. It's a full giggle. I've got something up my sleeve.

GARCIA: That's the way it is for me, too. It's delightful. It's fun.

MARY: Well, when will it be ready?

GARCIA: I don't know, I might be working on it for the rest of my life. Somewhere early in this next year, I hope. Maybe early spring. I think this next spring it should be done.

Interview With Richie Havens

MARY: In front of me today I have my friend whom I haven't seen in a long time – Richie Havens. Now, Richie and I have been sitting here giggling and laughing about the fact that we both started singing in the Village about the same time together. And about the incredible, wonderful talents that we learned from who nobody ever heard of. Because everybody heard about Bob Dylan and Peter, Paul and Mary and Bill Cosby and Woody Allen. All those people. We've all heard about those guys. And they were there. But nobody heard about the Hugh Romneys, the Len Chandlers, and Dave Van Ronk.

HAVENS: He gets known. Somehow or other, he gets known. I guess most people think of him as one of the pioneers, sort of bluesy, folk music.

MARY: Oh, I think so. Certainly for New York.

HAVENS: Yes, definitely.

MARY: Where are you from originally?

HAVENS: From Brooklyn. When I was in Brooklyn, there used to be a little syndrome going on called the Street Corner Group, like the Persuasions. The Persuasions personified my whole childhood. That's where I was at the whole time, singing on the street corners with guys. And being able to go to different neighborhoods and not get beat up. Because we sang together. There was a little group in every neighborhood. On every corner. That was sort of like the Underground Railroad that you could get through.

MARY: This is really the scene of my life, as well. I grew up not getting along too well with my peer group. And I found a peer group that wouldn't kick me out. And it was called music. You could always go to the park on Sunday and sing. Nobody said you had to go away. I mean, get out of here.

HAVENS: It's true.

MARY: I mean, I don't know how bad you sang or how bad you played, somehow the ticket was – Do you like to sing? Do you like to play? Do you like to be part of this thing called music?

HAVENS: Well, the music thing, as far as I am concerned, was my saving grace in Brooklyn. I grew up with music all my life. Once when I first started working professionally, a guy asked me, What were your roots? Who did I listen to? And I realized that my mother listened to country and western music from the time I was born 'til the time I was about 17, every day, and my grandmother used to listen to Yiddish music in the morning. And right after that it was the gospel music, with every ethnic kind of combination.

MARY: I've watched you on stage and there is a very, almost Old Testament quality sometimes, to your drama. You remind me sometimes, in Jewish folklore, there is a concept of the just man. As long as there is a just man, the world doesn't come to an end. Kind of the person who takes it upon himself – the pain. And you find it in many, many cultures. But I often think in a sense that the artist chooses to take upon themselves a certain level of awareness. A certain level of pain, and to try to minimize, not make it go away, because you don't want to make it go away, but you just want to explain it.

HAVENS: Music, very basically, even in the fact of learning to be a just man, music is very much involved. A very basic place. It's the ohms and the chants, and the singing and the drums. The drums being the first instrument coming up rhythm and a heartbeat being – that's why we like jazz, because our heart beats a little bit off. We never recognize these things. I kind of study these things.

MARY: You know, I think it's very organic.

HAVENS: Yes, organic and intuitional, I think. Something we don't recognize consciously.

MARY: I had a lesson in this once. We used to go around and sing in hospitals. And one day somebody got us into Bellevue Psychiatric Ward. And there was a young child, and I do mean young, like 5, who was in a catatonic trance. And we were singing. All of a sudden this child came out, looked at me, handed me a playing card, and went right back in. And I was just devastated. Because I realized that for a fraction of a second, the music and the rhythm and the feeling had pulled that child out. I didn't know how to react.

HAVENS: It's a curing factor. In music, there is something that water has also as a healing power. Music is the same in a less solid form. It flows, it knocks down walls. It can be just as hard as water, just as torrential, just as calm, as peaceful. It's very similar for me. But it's on maybe another dimension of playing, which we visit. And which visits us, which knocks down walls around us. There are people in my life that have been in that place.

MARY: Let's talk about some of those people.

HAVENS: Oh, God. There was a group called Heart Beats that later became Shep and the Limelights, the Diablo's, who made a song called *The Wind*, The Flamingos who did *I Only Have Eyes for You. Can You Dance?* by the Spaniards. We used to sing all of those songs. It was great. We had a ball.

MARY: I used to go to Brooklyn to the Henry Street Settlement House every weekend and square dance. And at this square dancing, there would be folk music. People used to get up and sing. Bob Gibson came. Odetta came. Lots of really professional people came.

HAVENS: We came up the same time.

MARY: But they were working. Then I used to sing in the park on Sundays. Roger Sprung, a banjo player, used to get the permit. Roger Sprung had the biggest record collection of anybody I know. That was the beginning. I never thought about it as a profession. I always thought it was a hobby. And something I liked to do.

HAVENS: Me, too.

MARY: One morning I woke up and it was my living.

HAVENS: Same thing happened to me.

MARY: I think a lot of people who start out, at least in music and art. I notice, for instance, there is an album of yours called *Richie Havens: His Portfolio*. And you have drawings in it. And I said to myself, there are so many. I started out as an art major. Peter Yarrow was an art major. Ian Tyson of Ian and Sylvia was a graphics artist. Ray Boguslav, who was Harry Belafonte's accompanist, was a graphics artist. There were more people that were involved in folk music at that time, who were also artists.

HAVENS: I think it was a more illustrative communication, you know, dimensionally coming too long or emotionally involved. And music was more vivid.

MARY: The artists that we have talked about – some of the people in the beginning – when I asked you about some of their records or some of the artists that you really liked, one of the people you mentioned was a woman who influenced me a great deal, too, Miss Nina Simone.

HAVENS: Oh, yes.

MARY: I remember going to see her at the Village Gate. Lots of times. And the energy, the commitment, and the anger that you used to feel from her – she sent out electricity bolts on stage. But I remember seeing her at the Selma Montgomery March in the nighttime. We were all terrified, but we were all joyous. Because we knew it was getting better. And I remember she sang that night in Selma, *Mississippi God Damn*, and it was the funniest night because she couldn't sing it mad. She couldn't put that bite, that nasty bite into it, that she always put into it, because she was laughing. Because we were all making it better. And so when you are making it better, it's very hard to spit.

HAVENS: It's true, it's absolutely true.

MARY: I'd like to play your *Just Like a Woman* back to back with Nina Simone's.

HAVENS: Great. That's a great song.

MARY: It's hard to explain, I think, to people who are not musicians, the place that you sometimes get to, where if you rehearsed, and you know your homework, you might get there.

HAVENS: You know, I tell you something, I think the Village in the old days was a million and a half magic moments like that — two people getting on the same stage and singing like that when they never sang together before. Places that people forgot that they sang together with each other. Len Chandler and Dino Vilante, Major Wiley, and Fred Neil all on the same stage.

MARY: Freddie Neil. I want to play a record of Freddie Neil's.

HAVENS: One of the first guys who inspired me to play the guitar.

MARY: And Freddie Neil is one of those unsung heroes, who sings good. There is nobody who has a baritone bass voice like him.

HAVENS: No one.

MARY: He has written some fabulous songs, some great lines. *The Dolphin* is a beautiful song. And he has done some, a whole bunch of wonderful songs.

HAVENS: That was the first guy I ever saw in concert on the stage at Hunter College. It blew my mind. I didn't even know how to act. It was a concert. I was going to see this guy sing on stage. It was really something. I had always been inspired by singing people on stage. When I was a teenager, it used to be rock-and-roll people. And now I was going to see the folk person sing, having been in the Village a couple of years, and a guy who I knew was saying something. He's going to tell me something. And I went there, and it blew my mind. It was really a beautiful experience.

MARY: Noel, or Paul, whatever you want to call him, Stookey, came to the Village from Birmingham, Michigan. He had been a rock-and-roll singer. He had a group called the Birds of Paradise. And someone said come to this concert at Cooper Union. There's this concert with Julian Bream.

HAVENS: Oh, yes.

MARY: Well. He took one look at that classical guitar player, took his electric guitar, sold it, bought himself an acoustical guitar and hid in his room. And figured out how to play.

HAVENS: You know what – he inspired me a great deal. In the beginning, when I first came to the Village, the first place I did go was to the Gaslight, because that's the one that was in the newspapers. I'd go there in the daytime and drink cider until night. So I did that. Noel did a song one time that I have never forgotten in my life. I mean this song has been an inspiration. I keep asking him to record it. I think he just did after ten years. *Dear Hands.*

MARY: Oh, yes.

HAVENS: Now that song he sang at Gaslight 12 years ago. I saw him sing that song. His arrangement of it was part and parcel of the melody of the way he played it.

MARY: It was a pretty song.

MARY: You know, it's funny. There have been performers that never happened. And I don't understand quite why they didn't happen. They were there at the right time for everybody else except the public.

HAVENS: Right. That's true.

MARY: Take somebody like Bob Gibson. You can hear his banjo in all of the stuff that the Limelighters did. A person like Shelly Silverstein, a massive influence to a great number of people. The rest of the world knew him as a cartoonist for Playboy. We knew him as a musician, as a songwriter.

HAVENS: There are a lot of people like that. Like people who have gathered up information and just happen to be around at the time when the people who want to transmit the information need to know it.

MARY: Right. Exactly.

HAVENS: They were our teachers. It's true.

MARY: I think it's always fascinating that what we are discussing is the fact that there are people who are not famous who make up famous people.

HAVENS: That's right.

MARY: And this happens all the time. They may think what they are doing is very minuscule or unimportant. I had a music teacher in high school – Bob DeCormier, who was later to become the choral director for the Harry Belafonte singers. He really loved music. He taught me the integrity of music. There's a wonderful line by Charles Ives, the composer. And the line goes, "A song has a few rights, just like any other citizen." And you are not supposed to tromp in there with your boots on.

HAVENS: That's true.

MARY: If you are going to get in bed with a song, take off your shoes and socks.

HAVENS: That's what actually creates the different styles of music. It's the fact that some of them are regarded as sacred and some of them are regarded as informational and some are just dance music. Some people go in on a song and they jump. Then the only thing you can do with it is dance to it. They just push it, just to the point where it's not beyond listening. You know, it could go beyond listening. It could go beyond listening and beyond dancing.

MARY: Where the lyric gets lost. Well, in the 15 years, well, 20 years, or 10, or 11, or 12 in the '50s, the words weren't so important. But it was always the melody was the whole thing. The musical value of the song. If you go further back to the Noel Cowards, where the words were important, Cole Porter, the melody was almost second. It was, did you have a lyric that was snappy? Then we went through a period of music where it was just the music in the '50s. And then when we hit the '60s, we went back to words again. And you could watch it happen between folk music. Then it was folk rock, then it was rock and acid rock. And then it went crazy. Completely. And now it's turning around again and the words are coming back.

HAVENS: It's coming back again. It's true. And they are much more mellow about singing and not pushing it there. They are sharing music again.

MARY: Another song, *It Could Be the First Day*, is a song of yours. Tell me how you wrote that.

HAVENS: It's strange. I write some songs from the music, the melody comes to me first. I may be riding in a taxi or something, and the melody will come to my head. The line will just come – singing the whole verse right through my head. Then I say, Hmmm … that's the verse.

MARY: Do you write it down?

HAVENS: No, I go home and play it, so that I know what I heard in my head. I have to match it up to what I heard. Basically, the music itself, the melody itself, tells me what the words are. The mood, what it's speaking about. What the original feeling was. Which is the music without words. I sat down

one day and wrote that. The melody came to me. It was
one of the first songs that I wrote.

MARY: Let's play the song. That's really the consummate statement —
to play the song itself.

HAVENS: *Inside of Him.* That's a song I wrote for Nina Simone, do
you believe it? But, I never got it to her. I don't know why.

MARY: Did you hesitate to send it to her?

HAVENS: I wasn't into business at that time. I didn't even know
how to get it to her. At the time I wrote that song, I didn't
know anything. It was in my mind to do it.

MARY: Well, we'll just say it's for Nina.

CHAPTER 9

Rhyme and Reason

Poetry was one of Mary's passions. In addition to avidly reading poetry, she wrote it, too. Below is a sampling of some of her poems.

The Sky Over Bleecker Street

Came downtown today
To Bleecker Street
To see the way
Feel the way
It used to be ...
On Bleecker Street.

Cold-water flat
Red wine
Friends and flowers then
On Bleecker Street.

And clothes strung out –
Love and hope for –
On our pulley-line.

Love and hope – for
Always on our pulley-line.

But there have been,
I regret to say,
Changes made …

Too many changes made …

So I come down again
To see the sky
Fair and blue
Over Bleecker Street.

Always fair
Always blue
When we were there
On Bleecker Street

When we were there
On Bleecker Street.

But a Moment

Memory moves us past each other.
Time is a ribbon without an end.
Love is the lesson we keep learning.
Death but a moment we must spend.

Last week as I made our lunch
We talked of yesterdays.

I remember more than you.
That happens lots these days.
But how we laughed, I almost cried
And the afternoon flew by,
As we sat on the patio sipping our drinks
And the sunlight began to die.

Memory moves us past each other.
Time is a ribbon without an end.
Love is the lesson we keep learning.
Death but a moment we must spend.

And we try to give each other comfort.
We try to hold off that dark night.
Each of us careful for the other
Keeping our own fear out of sight.
Ah, you know I've always loved you.
And I know you've loved me, too.
So it's hard to watch you crumble.
And forget all that you knew.

Yesterday while I was driving,
Sunlight streaming through the trees,
Suddenly my heartache parted
And suddenly I felt at ease.
You will love me all your life
As I will love you all of mine.
That's the gift we give each other,
That's the gift divine.

Memory moves us past each other,
Though time is a ribbon without an end.

Love's still the lesson we keep learning
And death but a moment we must spend.

It's Been a Hard Winter

It's been a hard winter for mom and her friends.
She went to a home, and for some, life just ends.
A whole generation, a century strong.
Taking our childhood memories with them, gone.

They grew up in the Great Depression,
Saw unions grow strong,
Fought in World War Two,
Thought that racism was wrong.

You were our compass,
Made history true, fought for our future.
Paid gladly our dues.
Now we trade places at the head of the table.
We pray that we, too, can be just as able.

Maturity

It's as if one has many births.
When I was little, they were spaced.
As time is when you are small
The eternity of summer
Then they seem to stop.

And the newness of life seems to pale
And for a moment you think
Ah,
This is maturity.

Don't get smug; life is just taking a breather
And getting ready to lower the next boom.
Then it's your children.
They, like small atoms of yourself,
Trigger their way to emotional fission
That startles you.
From any quiet lethargy you might have been contemplating,
And you sit and say,
But I am 28,
Grown.

Working on her poetry while on the road in Washington, D.C. (Photo by Maddy Miller)

What is this almost helpless inexperience I feel?
It's growing, says your own private sage.
Again, says I?
And I suppose you grow.
And they grow.
The inner voice cries out:
But it's their turn.

Faceted Crystal Flashing

Faceted crystal flashing,
Attracted by the light we turn to
Stare. Smiling we reach to grasp
The light to feel its warmth,
To somehow pull it, molecule
By molecule into ourselves.

Past the light, it is still a crystal
But peaceful in my palm.
There is too much stridency in me yet,
Softly and gently I sit it down
Knowing peace is not enough
But grateful for the moment.

Love

Love allows one to see others
With compassion.
Love makes the world a little safer.

Love allows us to know and
Understand fear and fragility.
Love defines and fulfills
The commandments.
Drink to love
Drink our love of you.

One Yesterday

One yesterday you carried me
And put dinner on my plate
And tucked me into clean sheets
And kept me safe for slumber.

When you became my child
I did not feel my womb stir.
But oh my heart went wild
To beat away my weakness
To make more room for you
To hold the love you gave me
So I could give it back to you.

We take small steps down long hallways.
I prompt our conversations,
Reminding you of memories.
Reminding me of them, too.

You do not seem to mind
Your loss and circumstances.
Your grace will dignify

Each elementary matter
As you prepare to move
Into a new dominion.

Notes From La Daliah

Fifteen fresh-dug graves;
The raw soil slightly sunken.

It was their first cemetery and
They had chosen carefully.
A nice hill
Not as tall as those that surround the village,
The ones the contras spilled over,
But well within the circle of their lives.
The community still whole even
In its grief and fear.

A large wooden cross marks the entrance.
Printed on it was the single word:
"Forgiveness."
In the earthen depressions
Left by an eight-year-old girl,
Fathers, sons, and mothers
Someone had planted red and white impatiens.

Simple peasant people of pride and passion.
A people with a new dream,
Of literacy, land, and freedom.

A dream big enough
To defy a sad history
And alien paid armies.

A small country where the children beg for pencils ...
Nicaragua.

My Mary

Mary and husband Ethan Robbins. (Photo by Robert Corwin/robertcorwin.com)

By Ethan Robbins

I asked her to marry me three times before she finally said "yes."

We first met when she came into my restaurant in the summer of 1981 with a group of her friends. We hit it off immediately and soon began dating. For 10 years before the wedding, we lived at her Manhattan apartment around the corner from Carnegie Hall, just across the street from the Carnegie Deli on Seventh Avenue, before we finally made the move to Redding, Connecticut.

Mary exposed me to her world of show business, art, literature, and social commitment. In our 28 years together, I was energized by her positive approach to life's twists and turns. She had the true ability to live life to its fullest, whether in the public spotlight or in quiet family times.

Mary's energy and enthusiasm were boundless when she was in full gear, from delivering speeches for causes she supported, to discovering a new culinary creation, to hunting for antiques in quaint country shops.

She was a voracious reader who was not limited to any single genre. While never without a book, she also loved daily newspapers and thrived when writing for them. When working on a column, she bubbled with enthusiasm, no doubt because it challenged her creatively and offered her a different forum to express herself.

When she was published, it gave a special sense of gratification, having stepped into the world of her parents' profession.

Mary's core ethic commanded she fight for life's promise of equality and social justice and to promote harmony and understanding, a dream that she would never let die.

When she fell ill, her fighting spirit was undaunted. On the back of our car she placed a sticker with the letters CCKMA – meaning "Cancer Can Kiss My Ass."

Our time together was blessed and magical. Our mothers became dear friends and our families warmly connected, expanding the sphere of hearth and home for us both. Her musical and political legacy is one of optimism and joy that will live on in those who share and for those who one day will learn her message.

Mary Travers didn't just change my life, she was my life.

Epilogue

Mary and I made an odd pair, she the first lady of American folk music and I a Vietnam vet who fought the war she protested.

My initial connection to the group was through Peter, whom I covered as a newspaper reporter in the late '60s. Back then, he was making headlines as an antiwar activist and organizer.

My relationship with Mary began in the early '80s, through Peter, when I was editor of the *Bucks County Courier Times*, a suburban Philadelphia daily newspaper. She was angry with a *New York Post* column that she felt was nasty regarding her hosting a luncheon at her Manhattan apartment for Nicaraguan President Daniel Ortega, who was in New York to speak at the United Nations.

The headline fueled her rage: "If I Had a Hammer and Sickle."

I told her to respond in kind, that is, write a response explaining her position and what she learned on her visit to the strife-torn Central American country. I knew that in fairness, the paper was very likely to publish it on the Op-Ed page. But after I worked as her editor on the piece, she decided not to send it to the *Post* but asked if I would publish it in my paper.

I did, and we were off to the journalistic races that lasted for more than 25 years.

Over the years, we worked on her columns, speeches, and essays. I tended to stay away from her poetry since I believe that form to be very subjective and should remain that way.

Our working together blossomed into a true friendship. She was no longer a writer or celebrity to me. From the time I attended her 50th birthday bash in Greenwich Village and her marriage to Ethan Robbins, through our shared vacations, to weekends spent together at my place in Bucks County or hers in Connecticut, our families became part of the dynamic. We would cook for each other and talk into the wee hours, sipping Irish whiskey and exchanging opinions on gardening, dogs, kids, and grandchildren – and, of course, writers.

One of my most poignant memories is of the afternoon she handed me old letters that her dad had written to her mom during World War II. "Mike, do me a favor and read these to me." I did, and she smiled as she listened to his instructions as to what Virginia should do if he didn't make it home. Her favorite parts were when he asked and expressed love for her, the woman he called "Bunny."

I vividly remember the day she stunned me with the news that she had been diagnosed with leukemia. She faced it bravely and, after more than a year's wait, with the best medical care, finally found a bone-marrow donor in Mary DeWitt of Lake Orion, Michigan. The transplant was a success.

"Renshaw, you won't believe it. The donor's name is Mary, too, but she's a Republican. I'm afraid when I go into the voting booth, my arm will shoot up to the GOP lever," she joked.

Buoyed by the good news, she talked about her condition from the stage and wrote about it:

> In the beginning of my many hospital stays for leukemia, I began to receive books on spirituality. They came from perfect strangers and some friends.
>
> I threw them all away.

Dismissive of religious self-help books, new-wave or old, I doubted they were going to help heal me. I wasn't quite sure what was going to work, but I put my faith in science. The mail and emails kept coming, and Paul Kehoe and Sally Farr, who worked Peter, Paul and Mary's website, compiled them into three-ring binders, finally ending at 27 books.

What they all had in common, whether they were prayers or just words of encouragement, was there was a world out there that had been truly touched over the years by Peter, Paul and Mary, and these people were reaching out and wishing me well. I was inundated by their care, and it changed me.

It might well have saved me.

Love and concern is a powerful medicine. In times of crisis, they reinforce the feeling that the patient is not alone, and that helps make the battle for health easier.

I can't say I've become a religious person because of this experience, but I must accept that prayer has an effect, and am grateful. I am grateful to my family for their love and unbelievable support, to my friends who kept me from having to eat hospital food and who made me think back on years of friendship.

I am so grateful to people I've never met, people who donated their blood; I consumed a great deal of it. Doctors who were artists and scientists. Who prescribed just enough chemo to back off the cancer but not so much to kill me.

Nurses whose humor and skill were ever-available. And the [then] unknown person who gave the bone marrow that courses through my bones now as if it had always been mine.

All that and the prayers. Do prayers need faith? I don't think so. Not for the recipient. I know that some prayers are fortified by faith and some are deeply felt hopes.

When did science and spirituality meld together to save me? I don't know.

I can only be grateful that both were in my life and that they were not exclusive of each other.

This was the last thing she ever wrote.

While the transplant was successful and left her cancer-free, the chemo and radiation treatments took their toll on her lungs and liver.

■

She would never say good-bye. "Not good-bye. . .to be continued," Mary always corrected.

And it will be continued in the ageless harmony of her musical legacy and in those who are inspired by her quest for harmony to strive to bring love, peace, and equality into their lives.

Mike Renshaw

Acknowledgments

Unending gratitude goes to Mary's husband, Ethan Robbins, and her daughter Alicia, who tirelessly collected archive materials and private photographs and enthusiastically worked to make this book a reality.

Also, this project would not have been possible without the energy of Peter Yarrow and Noel Paul Stookey and members of the Peter, Paul and Mary organization. Kudos to David LaPlante for preparing the audio of Mary's stage monologues and Tony Arancio for his reliable expertise in finding photos and answers to a plethora questions.

Insights from Shelley Belusar, the group's tour manager; Martha Hertzberg , the trio's manager; as well as musician Kevin Roth, who worked with Mary during the solo years, were invaluable. Recognition also goes to Mary's dear friend Rabbi Dan Syme, who supported and encouraged her journalistic efforts, as did her closest friends, Maddy Miller, Shelley Dowell, and Debbie Stallwood. Gratitude to Susan Painter and Fred Truntz for kindly providing the audio record of Mary's radio years.

From the world of newspapers, she was inspired and encouraged by author Christopher Wren, former foreign editor at *The New York Times* who fascinated her with recounts of his worldwide assignments and discussions about the craft of reporting. A special thanks to Bea Badner,

Mary's newsroom compatriot during the years she wrote opinion columns for the *Bucks County Courier Times*.

Thanks also go to Karen Wilson for her careful transcription work, Jeff Minton for his IT expertise, Ken Bookman and Kathryn Canavan for their learned publishing insights, and Steph Rosenfeld for his keen marketing advice.

And special thanks to Gina Renshaw, for her love, support, and understanding.

CPSIA information can be obtained at www.ICGtesting.com
Printed in the USA
LVOW04s2211091214

418088LV00012B/438/P